Praise for *Predicting Success*

"Dave Lahey absolutely understands the human dynamics of today's global workplace. He knows what mobilizing and accelerating a workforce is all about in the global battle for talent. Dave's thought leadership on the implementation of workforce analytics is the primer for the power of acceleration for leaders at every level."

— **Mike Stewart**, President and CEO, Predictive Group

"Dave Lahey has had many years working in and with some of the most successful companies in the world. In his book *Predicting Success*, he brings a clear and insightful framework to understanding the many and sometimes contrary dynamics we face in our business from day to day. It is this clarity that sets *Predicting Success* apart and makes it a must read for all managers who are looking for practical and useful systems and methodologies to solve business problems."

— **Robin Wood**, President, Predictive Advantage

"This is an easy read that concisely summarizes the unquestionable need for hiring tools in the success of any business (large or small). The book gives ample examples of the power provided by understanding your employees' skills and characteristics. The Predictive Index behavioral assessment tools and training not only transformed the way I ran my laboratory but also changed the way I approached teaching and mentoring my students and trainees, with the added bonus of saving a lot of money. In the end, the book highlights how these types of tools, available through Predictive Index, are really just a very efficient and cost-effective way of implementing common sense in projecting, planning, and executing management decisions."

— **Peter Backx**, DVM, PhD, Professor,
University of Toronto, School of Medicine

"David Lahey's book, *Predicting Success*, is excellent at helping leaders learn and grow. With his incredible knowledge and experience in business, Dave has this special talent to align challenges and people for higher achievements. It is not by chance that his company, Predictive Success, is definitely one of the most successful licensees in the PI Worldwide network."

— **Yves Djorno**, PhD, Strategic Coach
to Entrepreneurial Leaders

predicting
success

Evidence-Based Strategies
to Hire the Right People
and Build the Best Team

—

DAVID LAHEY

WILEY

Published by John Wiley & Sons, Inc., Hoboken, New Jersey.
Published simultaneously in Canada.

For general information about our other products and services, please contact our
Customer Care Department within the United States at (800) 762-2974, outside the
United States at (317) 572-3993, or fax (317) 572-4002.

Wiley publishes in a variety of print and electronic formats and by print-on-demand.
Some material included with standard print versions of this book may not be included
in e-books or in print-on-demand. If this book refers to media such as a CD or DVD
that is not included in the version you purchased, you may download this material at
http://booksupport.wiley.com. For more information about Wiley products, visit
www.wiley.com.

ISBN 978-1-118-98597-7 (cloth); ISBN 978-1-118-98599-1 (ebk);
ISBN 978-1-118-98598-4 (ebk)

Printed in the United States of America

10 9 8 7 6 5 4 3 2 1

To Patty

CONTENTS

CHAPTER 3
HOW TO LEAD
19

CHAPTER 9
HOW TO ENGAGE
127

CHAPTER 10

HOW TO RESOLVE

143

Contents

1

How to Start

PEOPLE. THEY ARE AT THE CORE OF everything a business does. How we work and communicate has been an area of study in North American corporate circles for decades. An avalanche of research describes an evolving global business landscape that will soon be populated by workers in jobs for which they are "mismatched," workers who live with an entitled view and disconnected workers whose skills aren't properly taken advantage of. These workers then must labor under the direction of so-called leaders whose own managerial talents are lacking a fistful of essentials—including the small matter of understanding how to get the most out of their workforce. Oh, and this is against the backdrop of weakening international economies, widespread unemployment, and spiritually bankrupt political players. Yoga breath now.

This is good news. This is what opportunity looks like. This is a chance for the tough to get going and the wheat to start drawing up separation papers for the chaff.

If everyone is thriving, after all, how can any single organization stand out from its competitors? It is from an environment of uncertainty and despair that the truly phenomenal emerge.

And better still, the trick to surfacing as the victor from such a challenging scene is a relatively straightforward one. Scientific in its proven application and even mathematical in its precision, employ it, and reverse your fortunes. Master it and never look back.

THE BLAME GAME

Job one on this pursuit is to gain an appreciation for exactly *what's wrong* with the status quo. Sometimes, business leaders are broadly aware that things aren't working so well at the shop, that resources aren't being utilized to their full potential, or that the lofty ideals they harbor for their company's existence are not being met. However, they're unable to identify the particular source of their shortcomings so that they might effectively address them. As per the adage, if you don't know what's broken you cannot find the solution.

If you're among those still wondering where the problem lies, here's a hint. It's North America's greatest asset, complete with an ill-applied skillset and an underused productivity well. It's the average worker, and you might think he's "just your mailroom supervisor" or "only your IT guy," but you'd be wrong. He's your entire company.

THE OFFICE PARADIGM, REVISED

Mercifully, long gone are the days when fat-cat corporate types would oversee a workforce whose participants inherently understood their role in what was. Looking back, it was a truly remarkable hierarchy. These were disquieting times. A pack of workers would toil their lives away, lining their boss's pockets — and nothing more. There was no sense that the individuals whose labors were earning money for the organization were anything but automatons, existing purely for the benefit of their employer. Their own personal objectives and quest for individual fulfillment were simply not factors. And the concept of work-life balance? Forget about it.

Still, it was a mutual arrangement, with both sides of the equation feeling kind of okay about the way things played out. I work for you. You pay me. You enjoy the spoils. I get the weekends off (unless the office needs me). Such noiseless tolerance for the status quo made exploitation easy. Managers could place extraordinary demands on their staffers who, in turn, would acquiesce without question. It was understood that bosses stood on the shoulders of their workers, but not with the same spirit of indebted gratitude as they might profess to today. In the old school, they perched without regard for the pain they were causing the guy struggling to stay upright beneath their weight.

Thankfully, a culture shift has since swept the workforce, and today's crop of managers is dramatically more enlightened than their predecessors. More than that, today's crop of the working class is more engaged with the value they bring to the communal endeavor, and more likely to make professional choices according to where their contribution is most appreciated and effectively utilized. Taken together, the latest generation of the North American working population possesses a much more sensitive appreciation for the human toll of sustained corporate success. I like to call this crew "the Facebook crowd." They demand to be treated uniquely. After all, they've been the subject of special attention all of their lives. Whenever I come into contact with these folks,

I'm wowed by their need for individualism. They want to be understood and to be seen as sources of light. They want the "big data" on their strengths. They want to know *who they are.*

There has never before been such a fierce need for human analytics in the workplace, and in work-life balance. The battle cry that human capital is the most important capital of all is ringing loudly throughout the land.

THE AWAKENING

It was a transformation whose time had resoundingly come. The world couldn't continue to function inside of an arrangement that rewarded one so unjustly at the expense of another—and still expect growth and success. The human piece. The future will be one where the number of jobs available will exceed the talent available. It will be a fight for "free agents," a path to find the best employees and also to keep them. The generation coming into the emerging companies grew up differently and has much less loyalty as part of its DNA. It will be "caveat employer."

Employment-granting executives must experience a dawning realization that they must find the right employee for their culture and either be hyperaware of employee discomfort with workaday lives or be ready for days, weeks, or perhaps even years in lost productivity—big time.

Sourcing, attracting, and training employees is an expensive enterprise, and if the inducted staff member proves a bad fit for the company once he's an established member of its ranks, well, the money's already been spent. In larger companies, you "hide" him by moving him to another role. After all, you can't admit an error because that would reflect badly on you. Sometimes you need to hire the "best warm body" to get that tick mark for yourself in the quarterly report. Who cares about hiring someone appropriate, just so long as you get that bonus, right? The employee will work it out. Never mind that he was wrong for the job. Never mind, either, the indirect costs associated with finding, interviewing, reference-checking, and onboarding the newbie. And never mind that the cash will now need to be spent again — to source and attract the next guy and bring him similarly up to speed.

On average, research from business information firm Dun & Bradstreet reports, it costs some $90,000 to attract, identify, hire, and train an employee whose managerial position pays $60,000. For a staff of 10 employees, that's $900,000. Still, it took an alarming amount of the world's time to come around to this reality and to finally pay this most critical ingredient of the recipe — considering its potential to impact an organization's fortunes — the attention it warrants. When a CEO sees the *real* ROI on preventing bad hires, it catches her attention.

THE COST OF A BAD HIRE

And so the first step to ensuring future success for an organization is to get a grip on the human resources that power it. Managers misunderstand the value of the individuals that populate their company break room at great risk and expense. Research demonstrating the cost of a mismanaged workforce — and the value of a well-managed one — abounds.

Certainly, there are direct costs that can be immediately measured — the most significant of which is an employee's salary and benefits. But it's in the muddy hallways of "indirect" costs that we run into trouble. Think loss of productivity; the expense associated with other staffers' recruitment, hiring, and recovery time; and the often considerable expenses of training a new employee for his assigned post.

The specific figures tracking the outlay of a bad hire for a company run the gamut, but all are sufficiently distressing. Estimates range from $7,000 for replacing a salaried employee, up to more than $53,000 for a staffer earning an annual salary of $40,000. The Society for Human Resource Management has suggested that replacing supervisory, technical, and management personnel can cost a company between 50 percent and several hundred percent of the individual in question's salary. The U.S. Department of Labor estimates that the average costs of a bad hire may "equal 30 percent of the first year's potential earnings." According to a report by the Institute for Research on Labor and Employment at UC Berkeley, turnover in management positions often costs 150 percent of the salary of the staffer in question. And another estimate — this one taking into consideration hiring costs, total compensation, the expense of maintaining the employee, disruption costs, severance pay, mistakes, failures, and missed business opportunities — submits that the termination of a second-level manager earning $62,000 a year in a position he's held for two-and-a-half years will deliver a bill to his company worth a whopping $840,000.

And outside of all these calculations is the intangible burden of discomfort with which a bad hire taxes a manager's psyche. Hire a guy who doesn't succeed on the job and endure a unique kind of failure. Sure, the flagging staffer pays the ultimate price in the loss of his employment, but the manager who brought him on board does not escape the experience unscathed. Thanks to such a misstep, the hiring process — and all the hoop jumping it entails — have to be endured all over again. The ad has to be reposted, the candidates have to be rescreened, the interviews have to be reconducted, the forms have to be rewritten, the introductions have to be remade, and the training has to be redone. And so on. Such an uncomfortable ordeal leaves a scar on every last soul who participates in it. An argument can be made that those managers with the better "golden-gut" intuition can do better in the selection process. But how much better? An interview is really only about as good as a coin toss in this game. Who knew that getting the right fit the first time matters as much as it does? Um. You should have. For most other "asset" purchases, you would have done your research and you most certainly would have "insurance" on them. A data-driven, people-founded asset plan makes business sense and reduces risk for any organization. Most managers do more research on the type of vacation they want to go on than in selecting the team whose labors will enable the time to have that vacation.

WHY THINGS FAIL

From the anxious marketing manager with a taste for attacking challenges aggressively to the retiring executive assistant who would sooner ask questions than provide answers, every workplace is awash in unique personalities. Assuming a personnel assemblage is made up of only like-minded characters, each with essentially the same needs, predispositions, and outlooks, is not only a lazy approach to human resource management, it's an erroneous one. Every last one of us travels with baggage; it's the clever business leader who can sort through the collection and make the smartest choices for how to best manage it.

And if you're still skeptical about the importance of marrying individual behaviors with both the task at hand and those that characterize the other players in an office environment, just ask a kindergarten teacher. She'll tell you it's a constant trick, finding the balance between one person's preferred ways and means and another's. My wife, Patty, has taught younger learners for years. She is a great teacher, in part because she realizes that her approach to each learner needs to be unique, and that there's less "drama" when the preferred ways are understood. Patty knows that in any of her classes she will have three camps: a group of "learners" who are sponges for knowledge, a group of "vacationers" who are in class because it consumes time between meals and parents, and a group of "prisoners" who hate school, hate process, and will always lead troubled lives. Patty has been able to pretty well predict, from among the tiny members of her kindergarten class, who will go on to post-secondary education with this "rule-of-three" process.

At the end of the day, by not persistently measuring every tool a prospective new hire brings to the table, and by not matching his skills, qualifications, interests, and personality traits with the work in question, an employer does himself a costly disservice. Every soul walks the planet in the company of his own particular set of gifts, after all. If his very specific properties are not aligned with the very specific efforts required of him in a job, then nobody wins.

GROUP THERAPY

But take heart, gentle executive. All is far from lost on this front. Indeed, managers just now coming around to this school of thought can take serious comfort from the fact that they're doing so in the company of legions. It's an apparent no-brainer, evidence notwithstanding, that the attention required of this subject at the corporate level is still emerging for the great majority of the business-based public. That managers are now acknowledging the need for staffers to be mindfully employed within a company, such that their talents and preoccupations — line for line — are put to the most effective use, constitutes a widespread awakening that promises to rewrite the corporate landscape.

Books are starting to be drafted on this subject and awareness is beginning to spread. Human resources departments are increasingly under enormous pressure to change. We're seeing emerging sectors in which talent acquisition is singled out from the reactive personnel roles in HR departments. We're witnessing HR leaders' push to get ROI education for their staff. And we're seeing smarter job descriptions being employed by better companies.

In turn, the world has responded with a slew of resources designed to smooth the transformation, making this a challenge that's — happily — very much in business leaders' control. A profusion of concrete behavioral science techniques exists to reduce the risk of a company suffering a talent shortage, and to maximize the payoff of an engaged and well-employed workforce. With a large percentage of employees "disengaged" (a Gallup 2011 study says 52 percent), any process that focuses on taking the employee from being a time consumer at work to a contributor at work is happily received.

2

How to Break Analysis Paralysis

SO-CALLED "ANALYSIS PARALYSIS" IS ONE OF those serendipitously rhyming terms that cleverly captures the characteristics of a condition from which a great bulk of us suffers—many chronically. Here we find an individual in the throes of an utter inability to arrive at a decision. Like a terrified deer caught in the headlights of an approaching truck, a person experiencing analysis paralysis is overwhelmed and immobile. He can advance neither forward nor back, so bewildered is he by the requirements he feels he must fulfill. Often, he remains in this state of inertia—casting about wildly for a sign that will clear the clouds and present an answer that makes conclusive sense—for much longer than the subject at hand could ever demand, all the while expending energy and time that could be applied to the much more productive pursuit of seeing through one or the other of the possibilities. And his peace of mind goes way south in the meantime.

Analysis paralysis can rear its hesitant head for every kind of decision, from what shoes to put on in the morning to whether to have a kid. And it's a frequent fixture in the business setting, where the affliction can be brought on from an excess of corporate bumps and corporately freighted, multilayered decision-making protocols. Too often in these scenarios, efficient determination about something is wholly unlikely because of endless, unnecessary discussion and evaluation. Studies are conducted, reports are ordered, meetings are held. And still no one is able to conclusively arrive at a verdict.

Indeed, more than individuals, entire companies can fall into the analysis paralysis trap. If the one for whom you work requires your regular attendance at more than two hours of meetings every week, you might be victim to this, the organizational strain of the condition.

Ultimately and at its tangled heart, analysis paralysis is a fear of the unknown. The absence of certainty of outcome can deliver anxious souls into fits of angst over the consequences of making a commitment to one side or the other without a guarantee of it being the more advantageous choice. And while it's perfectly natural to want to spend time thinking about a project, especially one that's freighted with an element of risk, there comes a point where any more thinking about it is counterproductive — the unknown be damned — and the imperative to start making some progress is pounding in your ears.

But there is a remedy for this unhappy condition. Indeed, there are a fair number of strategies for nudging the cement mental block out of the way and opening up the path for successful and satisfying decision-making, the participation of quibbling, detail-oriented, research-happy, ego-saddled managerial types notwithstanding.

Here are the best ones:

- **Make a mental commitment.** Sometimes, the best way to come to a decision is to make it—and then gauge your reaction to follow. In other words, you reach a conclusion by committing to something inside your head and then immediately taking stock of how this move feels. If your belly fills with immediate regret and despair, it could be you've made a poor pick. But if relief and joy are your kneejerk responses, that's better.

  In either case, be sensitive to the after-emotions of this approach. And be sure to fill in all of the details of the outcome, too, including the environment, the reactions of others, and the attendant financial benefits. Mentally replay your imaginary aftermaths over and over until you feel utterly confident in moving forward with one of them. Ultimately, you can take comfort from the fact that your decisions made via this approach are made in your brain alone. You've announced nothing; you've taken no concrete action. And so if you determine you've made the wrong one by way of your reflexive response to it, it's not too late to change. This strategy is useful, too, because it kicks fear out of the driver's seat to make room for the gut.

- **Act.** It's hackneyed and has been referenced into the ground, but the folks at Nike had it right when they urged the world to "just do it." Certainly you should spend some time pondering your various options. Tackle the age-old pro-and-con list with a vengeance. And, depending on the decision's relative urgency, sleep a night or two on the stuff and take stock of your clear-headed morning point of view. But then take your leave of any more indulgent exercises of decadent self-reflection and get on with it.

Put one foot in front of the other and take a step forward.

Now you're committed. May as well take another. Before you know it, you'll have put some distance behind you and the swirling quagmire that was your indecision. Better still, the satisfaction of having advanced from it will have fueled your confidence in your pick with each new step.

- **Change your decision perception.** A common view that people who are stymied by choice carry with them is one that imagines that there is really *only* option A *or* option B available to deliver them to destination Z. If they don't take one or the other, they fear, they will never achieve their endpoint, and they will forever have cut short their ability to do so. But what if there were actually many routes leading to the same goal? What if these stuck souls were able to imagine that, in fact, a great number of networked passages made their meandering way to Z?

  By recasting the visual in your mind as a web whose various threads provide for a multitude of means to the objective, it might free your mind from its perceived pressure to get it right in one.

- **Try CBT.** Cognitive behavioral therapy was originally devised to help treat depression. Here, unhealthy and dysfunctional thinking is directly replaced by more productive, nourishing thinking. Rather than train our attention on the past, this psychological approach focuses on what's wrong with our understanding of an issue in the present, and offers constructive alternatives for coming at it from a different tack.

  Most importantly, these arrive in the form of practical actions, such that a person trapped in a particular mindset is motivated to kick into meaningful gear.

By adopting the philosophies of CBT, an individual can discover fresh possibilities for recasting a situation in a new light that could never have surfaced inside of the penned-in enclosure of self-sabotage.

- **Fake it till you make it.** An entire school of thought bands behind the idea that, if you trick your conscious mind into feeling a certain way, it'll eventually be convinced that it *does* feel that way. For decision-making applications, this means climbing into one of the idling vehicles awaiting your decision, and taking it for a test drive. Charge around the city for a bit, ignoring any discomfort you might feel for the angle of the steering wheel or the depth of the seat. You'll get accustomed to this stuff and the ride will feel sweet in due time. Before you know it, you'll have faked your way through your emotional journey long enough that it'll feel authentic.

- **Set a timer.** Sometimes, all it takes to hit on a decision about something is to establish a deadline for when it needs to be made, particularly if yours is a personality that flourishes under pressure. In this way, you establish a clear limit to your information-gathering efforts that curtails an inclination to endlessly seek out that one last piece of data that will sway your conscience with certainty (and accept, while you're at it, that there will *always* be that one more piece of data out there awaiting your discovery). Oh, and don't be tempted to put your self-imposed deadline so far away that it floats in some distant future and lights no fire under your oversized indolence. Mind you, if you're the kind of person who regularly gets crushed under the weight of a time limit and you recognize as much, you might steer clear of this strategy and imagine, instead, that the timeline for your decision stretches endlessly into the horizon.

- **Seek outside input.** Decisions arrived at in solitude are not always the most wisely made. If there is someone familiar enough with your dilemma to offer a meaningful contribution to sorting through it, seek him out. And if your second opinion supplier has a personality that's a bit more, shall we say, reckless than yours, so much the better. Present your case to him comprehensively, including every detail of every argument, even the ones that make you squirm (especially the ones that make you squirm). Invite him to ask you questions along the way, and then poll him afterwards about which side he felt you exhibited the most conviction and qualification about. Remember that a display on your part of confidence and enthusiasm suggests a partiality to a particular point of view.

- **Have faith.** The most effective trick to busting through analysis paralysis is to adopt a trusting, Zen-like attitude to the whole thing. Reassure yourself with the idea that whatever happens is *meant* to happen. In this philosophy, there are no accidents or mistakes. The world is unfolding precisely as it should. If you embrace this mindset, you can release yourself from the crushing weight of responsibility. Fate's got this one in hand already, and so you can release your sweaty grip of it. And at the end of the day, take comfort that any outcome has to be preferable to the physical, mental, and emotional torment of your perpetual state of fear, doubt, and uncertainty.

- **Ask questions.** Sometimes the simple exercise of putting your concerns into words, and asking yourself to consider the entire range of considerations and possible outcomes that ensnare an apparent impasse can reveal the irrationality of your most deep-seated fears. Consider, for example:

- What do you absolutely have to do in order for this project to be a success?

- What could you realistically leave out and still have a reasonable chance of feeling satisfied with the outcome?

- What is the very worst thing that could happen if you choose option A?

- What is the very worst thing that could happen if you choose option B?

- **Break down your tasks.** Everyone who's ever made a list and included "make a list" as one of the items thereon understands the value of breaking a massive chore into a whole bunch of little ones. There's room for applying that same approach to the problem of analysis paralysis. Analyze the decision crowding your brain in its most minute detail. Divide it into discreet chunks or chronological steps. Then step back and, presto; a decision that seemed utterly unwieldy for its monumental hugeness is suddenly surprisingly, err, wieldy.

- **Seek professional help.** In extreme cases of analysis paralysis, a person might benefit from the participation of a medical practitioner to help nudge a profoundly immovable scene into action. Talk therapy sessions can uncover pathological explanations for an individual's rigidity around decision-making and offer therapeutic solutions for spurring them into a course of meaningful achievement. There is also research that draws a connection between analysis paralysis and depression, with a consensus that declares the presence of the latter in someone's psyche aggravates the presence of the former. In such cases, medications designed to even out a person's moods, boost his self-esteem, and reduce the drain of a negative effect on his productivity can prove useful. Moreover, studies confirm that the very process of making a firm decision can encourage more of the same in a depressed person. The unpleasant feeling of having no control is greatly ameliorated by the power that comes with sticking to your guns and watching the results.

- Analysis paralysis is an ugly condition that visits all of us at one time or another. When it strikes, it can leave even the most decisive of souls struggling to reach a satisfactory conclusion about something. In turn, picnics, birthday parties, and entire companies can be brought to their knees. Getting a handle on the stuff is within reach though. And every victory over it makes the next experience easier.

3

How to Lead

LIKE SO MUCH HACKNEYED BUSINESS JARGON IN the dictionary that drives the language of our corporate conversations, the word "leader" has suffered a heap of abuse that's left it swimming in misuse and misunderstanding. Hey, congratulations! You're a great individual contributor! How about being a leader of others? Along with this promotion, the specialist is often removed from a role in which she thrived and deposited in a role for which the training is in short supply and the path to learning leadership skills is characterized by self-discovery alone.

Leadership is sexy, looks great, and certainly brings more money home than the alternative. Egos get stroked at the top of the monkey bars, and the perks of such a charmed life all sound pretty appealing. So the individual contributor says yes to the new appointment. Now comes the challenge. Too many leaders have gotten stuck in the egoistic aspects of the term, so reveling in a lifetime's pursuit of the title of "playground lord" that they've lost sight of the other participants in the arrangement. Because if there's a leader, there are — necessarily — also followers. A leader with no one to lead is not a leader at all. A bully boss is no longer in vogue (if they ever were). Moreover, that is not a leader at all but, rather more likely, a future problem. The new leader is CEO of her unit and is armed with workforce analytics on her employees. She has evidence-based data on how to understand the drives and motivations and learning agilities of all her "assets."

And so, in its most facile characterization, a leader is an individual whom other individuals follow. And his prowess and proficiency in that task are what ultimately define him.

Jack Welch, the flamboyant former CEO of GE, knew this simple truth when he declared that, before you're a leader, success is all about growing yourself; but when you become a leader, success is all about growing others. And so it is that a good leader inspires not only the trust but the utmost regard of his nominal subordinates. She gets this with the ability to make "trust deposits" not "trust with-drawals." The leader is able to select employees and coach them uniquely. The leader today needs tools to assist in this journey. Hence the dramatic rise of workforce analytics. The leader today must get data on everything he touches, projects and costs, along with their impact on his people.

How he does so is similarly straightforward: by making choices that are appropriate for the entirety of the group over whom he presides. When he opts to take one path in lieu of another, he's doing so with the full knowledge that he has a trail of other souls in his wake. And he is ever mindful that the path in question must be desirable for the entire twisting serpent — and not just its tongue-spitting head. Because leaders, ultimately, are an organization's final arbiters, the guys whose decisions reverberate mean-ingfully throughout the layers stacked beneath them. In my work with hundreds of organizations, I consistently see that "people leave managers, not companies." So the bottleneck is here for productivity in human capital, full stop.

It's critical that a manager appreciate how vital this aspect of his role is. With his actions, a business leader endows an entire organization with value. And the more highly valued the outside world sees an organization to be, the more all of its members will be rewarded. Which delivers us back again to the most important element of the leader classification: his charge of those folks he purports to lead.

ALLOWING THE EMPLOYEES TO BE THE BEST VERSIONS OF THEMSELVES

It stands to reason that the most successful companies are those that are also the most productive. Each asset is used well, and any new dollar spent has an above-the-bank internal rate of return. A good leader can successfully extract the effort from his employees that will result in the most revenues sold, widgets made, accounts receivable collected, pages edited, and so on. Ideally, he is sufficiently in tune with his human resources to organize them in arrangements that capitalize on advantageous personality mixes, rather than lump together traits that clash and drag output down or, worse, create a climate of turnover whose constant requirement for on-ramping newcomers means productivity sinks. Simply hiring a person who fogs a mirror is about as risky as a walk on the state thruway or the Trans-Canada highway at night with no lights on.

Steve Jobs once told his managers that every extra second added to the process of logging in amounts to a cost to society of 4,000 man days a year. By applying similarly grand-scale mathematics to this conundrum, we can see that even a modest, five-principal operation that slashes the quintet's turnover tendency by a third can enjoy a 190-plus-day gain in annual productive time, based on a 200-business-day year. Business leaders, shrugging off another lost employee to a "bad fit" without really appreciating that a "good fit" is not only possible but essential, can expect to pay massively for this expensive oversight.

Imagine shrinking the time to hire by 30 percent, shortening the onboarding period by two weeks, and reducing turnover by between 20 and 30 percent? In my experience here at Predictive Success, the use of human analytic tools like the Predictive Index® (PI®) and Professional Learning Indicator® (PLI®) have delivered such returns for our clients. Evidence just beats opinion every time. When we remove bias in decisions in which people are involved, the process becomes one of validation, uniformity, and accountability to the business goals of the company.

If the company is looking to grow, there's no advantage to hiring leaders who are governance-oriented for the top of the house. If the company is in a maintenance stage and is happy with single-digit growth, it needs a more altruistic leader. If the company is on the market and looking for a buyer, it needs a leader who can contain costs and present the best picture as it pretties up the pig for auction.

So the business stage is vital in such considerations, as it sets the tone for the types of leaders required. The foundation establishes the script for the performers we need to execute on the show. As in a great play, the actors just "fit the roles." Better yet, they're surrounded by outstanding supporting casts and the logistics are all taken care of in what seems like a nonevent. The leaders "blend" and don't push, and the project gets done well. It's worth repeating: Leaders must *blend*, not *push*.

And so it pays, quite literally, for a leader to invest the time in understanding the personalities who work beneath him — both in isolation and combination — to get the most out of how their particulars might serve the company. With the right players on the teams, goals can be set mindfully—and with a realistic anticipation of achieving them.

THIRD-BOX THINKING

One Sunday last summer, our parish priest Rev. Shawn Hughes at St. John's Catholic Church in Gananoque, Ontario, delivered an outstanding sermon. The entire 45 minutes were centered on "being the best version of yourself." It really resonated with me. Imagine all workers being selected, coached, and trained with this mantra. A leader who can take the time to understand the goals set up for the group, and who can appreciate both that he will be under stress and how his factors of emphasis will play into the scene, will be able to lead better. And if this leader can stop and listen and think about the needs and motivations of those she leads, so much the better. Now you've got a scenario in which the manager is "blending" rather than pushing. This is what I call "third-box leadership," and this is where predictable success lies.

Specifically, "third-box" leadership describes one's ability to think about the impact of his communication on the other party. Instead of being a leader who barks out orders, the leader in the third box reflects for a moment on the behaviors and drives of the employee or colleague he is trying to influence. Our research with Predictive Index® data on employees shows that those managers who understand their unique levels of dominance, propensity for extroversion, patience, attention to detail, and decision-making style will make success more predictable. More than that, it'll bless him quicker, given his efforts to endorse a process that satisfies his leadership agenda to treat others as "they would like to be treated." This is "third-box" thinking in action.

When leaders demonstrate their commitment to their employees thus, the employees, in turn, tend to do that little extra on the job. The results can be dramatic. From my experience training over 4,000 leaders in this process who hail from companies like Microsoft, along with several national banks and many emerging high-growth organizations, it's clear that a leader's investment in becoming people-smart furnishes a competitive advantage. Indeed, one client wasn't pleased with my sharing of our human analytics approach to management as he regarded it as a best practice that I was revealing to the world. Which it is. Thanks to it, I've witnessed many companies populated by staffers who will go through the wall for their leaders and forget about the clock. These staffers do their tasks with more fun and less drama.

MEASURE IT, THEN DO IT

I hate poor service. In my management practice, I have the pleasure of eating at restaurants all across North America. On my travels, I make it a habit to watch the serving staff and predict the type of meal and eating journey I will experience. Ever have a meet-and-greet hostess who forgets to smile or sits you next to the kitchen? How about a waitress whose eyes dart at her other tables while addressing yours, doesn't welcome you, and forgets to ask how you like your food?

If the server in the diner across from your office is consistently unpleasant, it might not be enough for you to reflect your disappointment with his constricted tip. His personality may be so off-putting that it actually deters you from returning to the restaurant. This is not an effect confined to dining. Bad service may convince you not to return to a specific dry cleaner. Or car mechanic. These companies then wonder why business is so bad.

Why would the same scene not play out with your company, insofar as its human representatives' ability to influence the customers with whom they come into contact goes? Simple: it would.

It's critical that managers remember that the widgets or services they sell account for only one part of the overall offerings they tender to the world. The interface their flesh-and-blood agents present to customers is every bit as significant.

Enter human behavioral analytics. "What gets measured gets done" might be a hoary management doctrine, but no advice better highlights the connection between people's behaviors and the productivity levels of which they're capable. Managers who write this off as an unnecessary "soft" expense to which they cannot readily draw an ROI connection lose out.

After all, what other "soft" expenses is an organization otherwise bleeding money into? Maybe time lost to interviewing yet another slew of candidates or to handling safety issues that wouldn't otherwise arise if each employee was better suited for her responsibilities? What about training an endless stream of individuals brought in to replace the failures?

The best leaders use data to understand and motivate their employees (and to understand *how to* motivate their employees). By getting a fierce handle on the core behavioral strengths of every member of their team, managers can perfectly align them with the tasks at hand. This, as Jim Collins has long declared, is about the bus that is your business, and how to get the right posteriors in the right seats thereon.

Personality traits have been demonstrated to have a direct and substantial impact on job performance. Indeed, research indicates that between 20 and 25 percent of an individual employee's effectiveness on the job is actually attributable to his personality.

By employing scientific methods to identify achievers and producers, managers can then place them in positions that best exploit their God-given traits. Moreover, they can draw from these objective data continuously, and apply the ongoing training and coaching that will perpetuate this fruitful reality. Staffers will feel more engaged and usefully employed. Productivity will soar. Profits will rise. And everyone will win.

USING BEHAVIOR ANALYTICS TO PRODUCE A BETTER LEADER

Because an organization's success is so dependent upon the ability of each individual within it to perform at his personal best, it's up to the person heading up the lot of them to work toward achieving an optimal balance with their communal efforts by taking inventory of all the elements of their individual personalities. He could surmise such things, or guess. Better still, he could actually get a scientific account of them via bona-fide behavior analytic tools. As my friends at Google tell me, evidence beats opinion every time.

After all, wouldn't your life be that much easier if you actually had an operating manual on your staff members spilling over with clear instructions on how to handle each and every situation in which they might find themselves? With psychometric testing and behavior analytics tools, you do. Think of them as "radar detector detectors." There are many "tools" on the market today. The usual suspects include Myers Briggs, DISC, Colors, Herman Brain Dominance, and Hogan. These all have pedestrian appeal and have been present due to marketing efforts and the rapid licensing of their practitioners. A tool that has been one of the best-kept secrets—and one with a high degree of predictability and ease of use—is often not seen in the market. This tool is called Predictive Index®. I ran into this tool back in 1988 at a small printing company called McBee Systems Inc. We had our head offices in Toronto, Ontario, and Cherry Hill, New Jersey. The McBee Systems company's story was an interesting one. Somehow, they were manufacturing, marketing, and selling a manual accounting "one write" bookkeeping system very successfully across North America. I joined the company after taking the Predictive Index®. I witnessed the dramatic success the company had with the use of the Predictive Index® to hire all its employees—from commissioned salespeople, to operational people, to the folks who could be happy on a press for three hours a day while doing great, detailed work with actual engagement. These people used Predictive Index® from "hire to retire." The success was dramatic, and included great products with high gross margins and happy owners!

WHAT IS PREDICTIVE INDEX® (PI®)?

The Predictive Index® (PI®) is a theory-based, self-report measurement of normal, adult, work-related personality that has been developed and validated for use within occupational and organizational populations. Developed by Arnold Daniels in Wellesley, Massachusetts, in the 1950s, it has over 60 years of research and validation behind it.

The PI® is used for a variety of personnel management purposes, including employee selection, executive on-boarding, leadership development, succession planning, performance coaching, team-building, and organizational culture change, among others. The test employs a free-choice (as opposed to forced-choice) response format, in which individuals are presented with two lists of descriptive adjectives, both containing 86 items, and are asked to endorse those which they feel describe them (the "self" domain), and then those which they feel coincide with how they feel others expect them to behave (the "self-concept" domain). Summing across these two domains yields a third implied domain (the "synthesis"), which can be interpreted as reflecting an employee's observable behavior in the workplace. The assessment is untimed, though it generally takes approximately 5 to 10 minutes to complete, and is available in paper-and-pencil, desktop, and web-based formats.

The PI® measures four primary and fundamental personality constructs:

1. **Dominance:** The degree to which an individual seeks to control his or her environment. Individuals who score high on this dimension are independent, assertive, and self-confident. Individuals who score low on this dimension are agreeable, cooperative, and accommodating.

2. **Extroversion:** The degree to which an individual seeks social interaction with other people. Individuals who score high on this dimension are outgoing, persuasive, and socially poised. Individuals who score low on this dimension are serious, introspective, and task-oriented.

3. **Patience:** The degree to which an individual seeks consistency and stability in his or her environment. Individuals who score high on this dimension are patient, consistent, and deliberate. Individuals who score low on this dimension are fast-paced, urgent, and intense.

4. **Formality:** The degree to which an individual seeks to conform to formal rules and structure. Individuals who score high on this dimension are organized, precise, and self-disciplined. Individuals who score low on this dimension are informal, casual, and uninhibited.

The PI® also measures two secondary personality constructs, which are derived from a combination of each of the four primary personality constructs described previously:

1. **Decision-making:** Measures how an individual processes information and makes decisions. Individuals who score high on this dimension are objective, logical, and are primarily influenced by facts and data. Individuals who score low on this dimension are subjective, intuitive, and are primarily influenced by feelings and emotions.

2. **Response level:** Measures an individual's overall responsiveness to the environment, which is reflected in his or her energy, activity level, and stamina. Individuals who score high on this dimension have an enhanced capacity to sustain activity and tolerate stress over longer periods of time. Individuals who score low on this dimension have less of this capacity.

The PI® has been in widespread commercial use since 1955. Minor revisions were made to the assessment in 1958, 1963, 1988, and 1992 to improve its psychometric (psychological testing) properties and to ensure that each of the individual items on the assessment conformed to appropriate and contemporary language norms.

The PI® is currently used by over 8,800 organizations across a wide variety of industries and company sizes.

In 2013, more than 2 million people around the world completed the PI® assessment.

My experience has shown me that the data produced from exercises like that of the Predictive Index® will reveal whether a person is empathetic or analytical or assertive or tenacious or good with stress. They are entirely objective — a meaningful quality given the subjective influence of the manager from which it's spared — and therefore readily applicable to leadership-enhancement efforts.

If a leader is able to unleash the unique gifts of each team member and match those with the organization's highest priorities, success is sure to follow. Effective leaders recognize that it's folly to hire in their own image. They know that not all employees work the same way and that success is a function of adapting to this inconvenient reality. That means putting their employees in positions where they'll be able to best apply their inherent strengths. The tasks they learn quickly, the jobs they feel best about doing, and the talents they naturally exhibit should serve as powerful tipoffs to these.

As elementary a concept as this might seem, it's not one in widespread application across the corporate landscape. A more common sight? Business leaders honing in on personnel weaknesses and obsessing over means to fix them. One poll asking workers whether they felt they could achieve more success through improving on their weaknesses or building on their strengths turned up 59 percent in favor of the former.

None of this is meant to discourage leaders from following their instincts. For time immemorial, leaders have trusted their gut above all — and the tactic has worked pretty well. But validated, data-driven tools that mine the specific attributes of an individual supplement that intuition nicely with science. Taken together, the leader can make more mindful choices for his employees, who can look forward to feeling more precisely utilized and more fully engaged. And increased productivity and profit are the sweet by-products of it all.

EFFECTIVE FEEDBACK IS A SECOND PAYCHECK

The best leaders have a vision. It may be the wrong one, but they tend to know where they want their group to go. My experience has shown me that employees often have scant understanding of the strategy and direction of the company for whom they work. Sure, they beaver away every day on solving customer issues, closing deals, and putting out fires, but they otherwise exist in a professional vacuum. Worse, their employers keep them in the dark by reserving feedback that might otherwise have illuminated the scene usefully.

The best leaders are active in their responsiveness to their employees' efforts. Rather than limit their commentary to official reports, whose dense contents are too often so intimidating that few even bother to read them, they engage in regular, effusive, and *direct* feedback with those employees in their keeping. Such touch points are the first step to effecting behavior change within an organization.

Courage to deliver the tough message in the appropriate manner for each employee is essential. Given that talent has the ability to leave a company almost any day, it's undeniable that this asset is truly the most mobile. And the best leaders are genuinely interested in any process that can reduce the risk of employee "leaves." They know that treating each staff member with the gift of communicating to them in "their world" makes sense and builds "trust deposits." When we take the time to think about the people we are trying to motivate and how to best communicate from their personality we get a "trust deposit." When leaders forget this process or are not self-aware and com-municate from their world, they make "trust withdrawals."

Thinking leaders take the time to understand, study, and process the personality of the employee they would like to influence. Better leaders for decades have known that this just makes sense. When the leader understands the drives and motivations of his employees and pauses to use these in the communication events each day, it is like giving that employee a second paycheck each week, at no additional expense to their cost centers.

Best-in-class organizations might even employ systems — such as business metrics in a dashboard that are updated daily — to monitor the regularity of such efforts. Or maybe the manager just applies sticky notes to the desktops of his underlings that celebrate an achievement or acknowl-edge an endeavor. Either way, employees working for such engaged-with-them leaders respond, meaningfully, to feed-back.

Deciding to notice your employees' efforts, on however small or large a scale, is a choice leaders must make.

DO AS I DO

The most effective leaders know that, to get the best from their people, they need to effusively demonstrate the best of themselves. That means not acting simply as the head of a team, but as one of its most productive members. It means communicating your wishes clearly and going one better by actually *demonstrating* what you're looking to get done. It means that you must always keep your promises and do what you say you will rather than rely simply on the strength of being the boss. And, finally, it means following all the rules, because they're there for *everyone*, not just for the guys without the couches in their workspaces.

And the spin-off benefits of such behavior are considerable. By demonstrating consistency between what you say and what you do, you've given your staff an effective role model. More than that, you've given yourself an enhanced opportunity for success via the fuzzy feelings your people experience for you. If your subordinates believe that you're honest and straightforward, they'll be more inclined to trust you — and to believe their trust is well placed.

And so for all the idea-du-jour talk of so-called servant leadership, it's useful to remember the power of simply rolling up your sleeves and diving into the dishwater. Action speaks volumes. And an executive's contribution to a company-wide task sends a message that he considers himself equal to his employees — a valuable one for spurring morale and achievement.

EVERYONE'S A LEADER

Because leadership doesn't just live at the top of the food chain, it's important to make room for it at all the stops along it. Lots of people have leadership potential, regardless of where they happen to dwell on a company's totem pole. And it serves an organization's entire population well to explore which individuals possess this promise.

A shipping clerk who identifies a way to eliminate a step in an arduous process is demonstrating leadership tendencies. So is a receptionist who recommends a better means of communicating group-targeted information. And an HR leader who sees the business benefit of proactively using human analytics to look for patterns in accident rates in technical, sequential, high rules-based roles will undoubtedly bring business value to the company.

By exercising to its full potential the capacity of each individual within a business to broaden his professional existence into a leadership role, a manager cultivates a situation in which both sides of the equation feel purposeful and well employed. The staffer gets to fulfill his personal career aspirations, and the organization gets to dip into his talent pool for its very accessible riches.

Indeed, management experts at Wharton and McKinsey say that leadership can be found and must be practiced by employees at all levels of an organization. That is the only way in which an enterprise can get the most from managers and employees alike, achieve its strategic goals, fulfill the professional goals of its people, and lay the groundwork for identifying and developing future leaders, including those who may eventually serve at the highest levels.

CULTIVATING PRINCIPALS

Everybody can lead at every tier, from frontline to top line. Leaders are made, we've long known, not born. None among us enters the world endowed with those biological advantages that will better prepare us to guide others. Indeed, the essential set of skills for a senior executive — long acknowledged to include character, integrity, strategic-thinking powers, and decisiveness, among others — might describe any thriving professional occupying any spot in a company's ranks. Because while it's true that certain people are simply better communicators, have more booming vocal talents, or more persuasive powers of argument, the real skills of leadership are acquired over the course of a lifetime. And the chief of a company makes a conscious decision to seek out those individuals poised to put such attributes to work to the ultimate betterment of all parties.

The next step might be as simple as making reading materials on the secrets of effective leadership readily available to these individuals. Or engaging them in spirited conversation along these lines. More formally, a manager might directly inquire of a staffer what kind of challenges he might enjoy in his professional evolution. Or he might establish a leadership-development or -mentorship program at the office, whereby staffers are set on a specific path or paired up with superiors according to seniority and expertise.

The introduction of science-based data like those revealed by the Predictive Index® allows leaders to truly find diamonds in the rough. With such data, workers who might otherwise have been overlooked for development can be considered for roles that align with their core drive and motivation. Using Predictive Index® data, I've seen a major national telecommunications company stop hiring the cast-offs from the competitors and create its own models for success based on assertive, collaborative, fast-paced, and "cutback-detail" benchmarks. This has lowered its costs and created an evidence-based, predictable, and nonsubjective process for selecting employees.

By celebrating leadership tendencies in folks who aren't nominally leaders, a manager endows them with a tremendous sense of ownership and encourages a healthy spirit of collegiality, trust, and a mutual regard for performance across the organization. What's more, this approach scores an essential of successful businesses: perpetuity. It's generally recognized that if you're keen to retain talented junior executives, you have to give them opportunities to grow and develop. If someone's languished for too long in a particular business unit, shift him to another. If he's mastered the skillset required of a line position, try him out in a staff role.

Additionally, if you want to keep people, you must allow them to be that best version of themselves when they come to work. The data-proven, science-based program that is

Predictive Index®, in my experience, has allowed people who are normally not assertive to take on leadership roles. Knowing your core strengths and, equally, those areas in which you suffer gaps can only help to accelerate movement into new functions inside the business plan. I have worked with leading companies that use the Predictive Index® as their engine to not only hire the A players—but to keep them. Successful organizations like Salesforce.com, Hertz, Caterpillar, and Microsoft all use this predictive-modeling software to set their employees up for success by establishing appropriate role benchmarks with what is called the PRO® or Performance Requirements Options®.

And this education doesn't just take place with these leading firms' HR teams, but is extended to the line manager teams such that everyone can draw on the evidence-based data obtained from Predictive Index® to truly map each employee's assertion, analytic/persuasive paths, patience levels, and formality orientation. The data are rich with insight and allow managers to move to coaching with tenacity when needed.

NATIONAL TELCOM COMPANY EXAMPLE

A great example of leadership development in action can be found in Michael Weening, now a senior executive at Salesforce.com. Weening, a former high-potential staffer at Microsoft, eventually became a global business-development leader for the company. What we would call a rainmaker, Weening always delivered success to his employees and organizations and was famous for his comment, "I have ridiculously high expectations."

When Weening accepted the role of vice-president of the business wireless and consumer direct sales arm of a national telcom, with offices coast to coast, he pledged to invest in results-oriented training, employee-development programs, and management effectiveness to produce high-performing sales teams. To see this through, he called in big guns in the form of the Predictive Index® (PI®) and its companion instrument, PRO®. Group analytic studies of Weening's 583-man sales team led to the creation of a logarithm of the behaviors and drives of his top 100 and bottom 50 sales representatives. We also used the PI® to create a coaching-for-growth plan. Success in this commodity space arrived in year one, with core sales up 9 percent and higher-margin data sales up 38 percent — both huge returns for the human analytics spend.

At the time Weening joined this Telcom, less than 1 percent of staffers had personal-development plans in place; post PI®-implementation, this number had swelled to more than 85 percent. Many of his employees call Weening their "best boss," a reference to his choice to lead from *their* world, not *his*.

"The PI® training process served as a great team-building exercise," Weening says. "I wanted to help my managers get insight into their people and start to understand how to build out great development plans. To accomplish this, people needed to understand themselves and each other. The PI® can expertly help people recognize their strengths and weaknesses and then enable them to effectively articulate their needs to their managers and build out a realistic plan for success."

Both the PI® and PRO® tools are now best practices for the Telcom. And in 2012, Weening was approached by Salesforce.com to deliver his human analytics–founded recipe for predicting success to another growth-hungry firm. Again, data was his friend and brought a new evidence-based process to enhance the growth of his organization.

With these smart job-assessment and training tools and the robust information on individual behaviors and

working styles they uncover, team dynamics are strength-
ened, communication is improved, and performance is
boosted. Their employment means a management team
can define the behavioral characteristics needed for
success in a particular position and then clearly determine
the fits and gaps required to improve a company's staffing
landscape.

MORE THAN MONEY

Good leaders are rare and exceptional creatures. Possessed
of sufficient confidence, communication skills, and character, these folks are just as blessed for a personal attribute
they possess in lesser degrees: namely, ego. Too many of the
world's ferocious corporate scandals can be tracked back
to a swirling pot of unchecked ego (often boiling without
the mitigating effects of ethics). Too many leaders do not
acknowledge the damage of which this deadly sin is so particularly capable.

But by presenting a clear message, and backing it up with
powerful actions, impressive managers of such companies
as Microsoft, Tesco, Best Buy, and Walmart have rallied
employees to their cause and enjoyed bottom-line success
as a result.

Only by identifying — and communicating — a corporate
mission predicated on a communal set of values can a
manager expect to engender the critical spring into action
and necessary loyalty from her staffers. And nobody's
even mentioned a thing having to do with remuneration.

In my experience, it's simple-minded folly to imagine
that money alone is the sole source of motivation feeding
an employee's allegiance to his employer. Many studies
place money as number four on the top five reasons
employees are disengaged. Don't get me wrong: You

cannot pay your people peanuts, but money isn't the top reason people leave companies.

It's an age, after all, during which human beings' attention to their own personal journeys on this planet is a recurring theme inside our collective psyche. When I'm asked to deliver guest lectures in the MBA class of the two schools with whom I work, I'm consistently amazed by the huge appetite that young people have for personalized data. After my talk, the students will frequently wait a long time to ask for a personal debrief on their own Predictive Index® surveys. They are great learners in their favorite subject—themselves. And why not?

SELF-DEVELOPMENT RULES

Moreover, how could such preoccupation not spill into the professional arena? How indeed, asked international assessment and development consultancy firm Cubiks recently, with a survey that uncovered precisely *how important* the availability of self-development opportunities is for today's workers.

In a bid to gain insight into the experiences, preferences, and outlook of the contemporary international workforce regarding feedback, development prospects, and talent-management opportunities that await them in the workplace, Cubiks sought the views of some 500 international HR and non-HR professionals from 33 countries. Among other findings, the research revealed that the chance for an individual to improve himself on the job through self-development initiatives offered by his employer outranks even a pay raise in its significance for keeping him happy at work.

Specifically, a full 93 percent of respondents said they would stay longer with an organization that invested in their development than with one that didn't. What's more, in excess of 70 percent said they'd prefer getting training courses to getting more holiday time, and more than half said that they'd choose development opportunities over a pay raise. Amazing. Education is both welcomed and provides valuable ROI.

In addition, the research found that, while 60 percent of respondents find their line manager's suggestions on how to improve performance in their development areas useful, only 25 percent actually receive feedback outside the formal review process. Less than half of respondents reported that their company has a talent-management program in place. How often I still see performance reviews "jammed in" a week prior, when a manager had 200 days that year to schedule them, always catches me by surprise.

The survey singled out certain development activities among respondents' preferences, particularly emphasizing those that included interaction with colleagues or trainers. Coaching came out as the favorite on this front, while on-the-job training was identified to be the most effective. Face time with the boss is much appreciated but too often ignored or poorly used with employees. This is where we need the human analytics data to get to pay dirt quickly. Your perfect-pick worker needs to be shown how special she actually is. Data is the pathway to show you care. The Predictive Index® roadmap, from my experience during my time working with Microsoft, saved me hours and showed my team I was invested in getting to know them. The training event became not a burden, but a destination of discovery.

LISTENING TO THE RESULTS

The notion that populating your ranks with workers who are well suited and well prepared for their position is not a novel one. It's why behavior assessment so frequently surfaces as the smart and valuable management strategy it so evidently is. After all, if the people doing the work aren't happy with their lots, it's unlikely the organization for which they toil will thrive as it otherwise might.

But such miracles don't happen without mindfulness. An employer seeking a workforce made up of fulfilled souls needs to invest time and energy into making them so. That means listening to the results of surveys such as these — and responding with programs that seek to cultivate a culture in which staffers feel nurtured and appreciated.

THE LEADER AS INTROVERT

Society's assumptions notwithstanding, the most effective leaders are not always the loudest, most assertive, most outgoing people in the room. Research on leadership and group dynamics led by Adam Grant, an innovative professor at the University of Pennsylvania's business school, Wharton, takes direct aim at the conventional conviction that leaders have to be card-carrying extroverts to be good at the post. Indeed, they discovered that the reserved and retiring personalities are actually, in certain situations, better suited to the task of leading than the brash and bullish. What determines success here, they maintain, is tied up in the personalities of the people being managed.

The researchers discovered that pairing extroverted leaders with similarly gregarious staffers can make for a bad combo, for the sparks of friction that can result. And so too can the mix of introverted employees — "low Bs" — and introverted bosses, for the spectacular display of idleness this matchup is likely to produce. But the research they developed, eventually published in the *Academy of Management Journal* with the title, "Reversing the

Leadership Advantage: The Role of Employee Proactivity," reveals that there's actually a very worthwhile marriage to be found with an introvert at the head. Introverted leaders lead solely from an analytical point of view — and this can actually be an advantage.

Based on surveys from 57 units of a nationwide pizza store representing the experience of 374 employees, and having controlled for the average order price and worker hours, the study invited leaders to gauge their own degree of extroversion, and employees to rate the levels of proactive behavior they witnessed in their store. The results suggest that proactive employees are best led by introverted managers and that non-proactive employees are best led by extroverted managers.

Extroverted managers, hungry for attention, might thwart employee productivity out of discomfort and produce a culture of fear around employee initiative. Introverted managers, however, can make a good match with enthusiastic subordinates because they're inclined to listen to suggestions and support proactive efforts.

This inverse relationship has implications for business arrangements of all stripes. Failure to pay attention to such essential personality traits can lead to serious productivity losses and outright conflict. Managers should examine their own leadership styles and consider whether, sometimes, pulling back from the fray might be the most effective ploy for stimulating input from subordinates. This is not unlike the Fortune 500 CEO who endorses a policy of personal silence for the first 15 minutes of meetings. In any event, managers would do well to consider the makeup of the teams that operate beneath them, evaluating the leader-subordinate mix in terms of personalities instead of the usual skill inventory alone. Take a chance and pair extroverted leaders with less energized employees and introverted leaders with staffers who have demonstrated resourcefulness and drive. You'll no doubt be pleased with the experiment's results.

━━━━━

USING WORKFORCE ANALYTICS TO FIND YOUR NEXT LEADER

Whether a company owner's plans to sell or move on are imminent or distant, the imperative to identify the organization's next leader is an always pressing demand. To that end, it's essential for the current leader to qualify those personality criteria that describe the ideal successor according to his vision for the company's future.

Given that one-third of the companies in the S&P 500 Index and some 35 percent of the players on Canada's top best-managed lists are family-run operations, it's important to include them in conversations about succession. Indeed, it's often these companies — started on a bootstrap by a father and son or a pair of siblings — that are particularly in peril of stumbling at torch-passing time. Often, next-generation managers are chosen by dint of bloodline alone, and they quickly prove themselves entirely ill-suited for the job.

The once-thriving Eaton empire (remember it?) didn't stumble into bankruptcy in a mere three generations simply as a result of the exterior economic climate, as business profs have long pointed out to their students. This family is hardly the only one that has failed to see the importance in critically evaluating personnel personalities. Indeed, research has demonstrated that fewer than 30 percent of family businesses even reach third-generation status, responding as they do to family members' wildly conflicting approaches to money and management. It is troubling to see that family-run organizations continue to repeat this mistake. It is interesting to map out the personality of the founder of a company and watch what happens as a result of his success. The founder who is successful, is most often an assertive, fast-paced, tenacious "ambivert" with just the right amount of detail to advance his plan. From my experience, the fruits of his hard work can create a sense of entitlement for the offspring if not carefully managed. The offspring can lack that same sense of drive and urgency, and this can be apparent in their personality by the age of 19. The end result is a business with a succession problem. The founder had unique drives to build, and the offspring are more likely to be maintainers. Thus, we have seen the slow decline of many North American family-owned and -managed companies.

Family businesses fail for many reasons, including family conflicts over money, nepotism leading to poor management, and infighting over the succession of power from one generation to the next. Many of these problems can be handled better with personality profiling of the key members. Behavioral assessments of those potential leaders-in-waiting will reveal the truth.

Objective, evidence-based, data-driven human analytics offer information for assessing the behavioral strengths and weaknesses of individuals in the running for successorship, and comparing them to identified future models ideals. An examination of a family member's personality is every bit as valid as that of an outsider's. Such an exercise will frequently uncover that the entrepreneurial drive and furious work ethic of the father was not replicated in the son. I witnessed this recently in a large national company with whom we work. The father was an assertive innovator; a vision-setting person with a tremendous gift of velocity in decision-making. His eldest son was a harmony-seeking, analytical, and sequential person. Sound the bad-mix alarms.

Finally, part of the succession consideration is appreciating at what stage the organization is in its lifetime. A bushy-tailed startup, after all, is quite a different beast from a mature long-timer in its sunset years. The early-phase successor might be a risk-taker with a flair for innovation. The late-phase successor might be a consistent laborer whose even temperament and stomach for enduring effort would serve a useful role.

4

How to Follow

IT'S ONE THING TO KNOW HOW TO LEAD. It's quite another to know how to follow.

For as long as there have been leaders, there have been people bringing up their rear. This many years into the bargain, the dance is well-established: leaders set the pace, lay out the expectations, forge the path, and bask in the glory; followers do the heavy lifting, work in the shadows, make grunt wages, and take the heat. Two sides of the same ancient coin, each needs the other ferociously.

Leading is the celebrity role that catches all the klieg lights. Following, assumed to be a given in the wake of the path-setters, is every bit as key. Just as losing a race with grace is as important as ending it in civil victory, understanding the art of following someone else's oversight is as essential as mastering the qualities that define a great leader. Indeed, it might be argued that it's even more of a challenge to follow than to lead, particularly for personalities that are naturally given to taking charge and egos that flourish in the spotlight.

But even leaders must appreciate that it's neither prudent nor realistic to expect that they can call every last of an organization's shots. Moreover, they should understand that their comfort with taking direction from another is directly correlated to the likelihood that their company will enjoy success.

WHAT THE BIRDS KNOW

Skeptical? One need only cast his eyes heavenward to take a lesson from a winged collective and their approach to following a frontrunner. Canada geese travel in V-shaped formations on their annual forays up and down the continent. It's a sensible arrangement that sees the lead bird assuming the role of guiding his fellow fowl along a certain path while helping reduce the air drag that would otherwise inhibit the lot of them from covering the great distances they manage. Scientists have found that, when geese fly together in this style, they can cover 70 percent more distance than if the birds were to fly alone.

The configuration also ensures that the flock distributes the workload sensibly. Because the task of leading one's feathery cohorts across vast spaces and negotiating the considerable wind resistance that comes with that air-busting front spot is an arduous one, it would be madness to imagine a single bird could do it forever. Such it is then that these clever airships trade the yellow jersey regularly over the course of their flight, the leaders signaling the factions of their intention to make a shift, and then gracefully falling back into the corps to allow a fellow flyer to assume the front-flying role.

As with so many other examples in nature, the Canada geese's behavior provides an excellent illustration of an equally vital principle for the successful operation of a professional organization. Study the migrating birdies and learn much about how to approach leadership and team collaboration. Again, evidence beats opinion every time.

Leaders must understand that theirs is a fluid position, and that the time put in in the ranks, efficiently responding to another guide's instructions, is every bit as important as the time at the front of the pack. It's in this way that everyone on a team gets that everyone else has his back, and can feel reassured that the shared workload will mean no single member wears out before the group as a whole reaches its objective.

Managers focus on work, they say; leaders focus on people. Some of that focus finds its feet in granting more responsibility to employees. By clamming up and letting their voices ring out, a leader speaks volumes about his confidence in his people. They feel puffed up, in turn, and everyone scores.

███████

FOLLOWING TYPES: PEOPLE STYLES MEET THE FACEBOOK CROWD

Nevertheless, the world perceives the act of following negatively. If you follow, you're presumed to be passive, weak, and too lily-livered to claim your own square of turf. But this representation describes a particular *kind* of follower—the guy who takes direction without question and is likely too lazy to ever stir himself into any kind of precedent-setting action. Social styles describing such personality types have been around since Carl Jung set them in motion. The ability to understand that people in business tend to fit a bucket of personalities is data that leaders need to be aware of and use for leadership growth. Jung's research determined there are four styles of people we need to understand. He found that each of these four

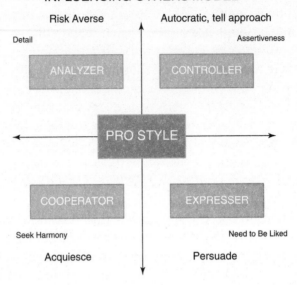

Figure 4.1 The Influencing Others Model

needed a unique and different approach to influence action. These are: Analyzer, Controller, Cooperator, and Expresser (see Figure 4.1).

There are other follower types, however, and not all suffer the same unflattering portrayals. A recent *Forbes* article identifies five types of followers, and points out that, just as there isn't a single defining ingredient in all leaders, followers have different provenances, too.

THE HIERARCHY-FREE IDEAL

Integral to communal success is a person's ability to relinquish the reins to another and to selflessly accept his occasional role as disciple. The notion of such an arrangement has been seriously floated among corporate circles. A thoughtful movement considering the merits of the so-called bossless office has gotten serious traction of late, and its influence is evident on the business cards of a generation of managers that call themselves such equalized and authority-busting titles as "chief fun creator" or "co-poobah."

In these utopian scenarios, coworkers purport to "manage each other," pulling collectively in the same direction without any one of them holding sway over the other. In the extreme version of the ideal, staffers make every decision about their own working lives, including which projects to pursue, when they take holidays, and even how much they earn.

Such a level organization, say its proponents, encourages individuals within it to work harder than they otherwise might, so cognizant are they of their part in the big picture. Without the looming and inhibitory oversight of a supervisor, people toil more freely. Further, they take responsibility for tasks they might have avoided, because the unfettered opportunity to do so excites them. Released from the overbearing demands and constant review of a manager, individuals explode into action and deliver productivity in great heaving waves.

In theory.

While certainly appealing on some level, the practical reality of such self-managed working groups is rife with potential for trouble. For one, there's the risk that decisions that have to be made never are, in the absence of a buck-stopping soul who might insist on it.

For another, there's the fallout from a frustrating absence of a target for on-the-job vexations. At least when there's a kingpin at the top of the field, the workers can find communion in their regard for this person as the common enemy. Without an immediately apparent scapegoat for their professional woes, a villain at whom they might direct all their delightfully mutual aggravations, workers can lose sight of their target and scattered incompetency can be the fallout.

And then there's the risk that employees will ultimately feel more burdened in their bossless office than they might have otherwise. With no official executive charged with policing the work lives of their nominal peers, an entire office full of conscientious folks steps up to the task. The result could be a company seething with pissed-off employees who all feel scrutinized by everyone else. Suddenly, the entire staff imagines themselves entitled to be tracking your comings and goings, marking the occasions of your tardiness and absence, and creating an unpleasantly oppressive working environment for you and yours. In an organization without a nominal leader, it's as accurate to say *everyone* is a leader as it is to say *no one* is.

None of which even delves into the challenges that such management-free organizations face when it comes to establishing an overall vision to guide the vessel through crowded waterways. And what about practical consider-ations like who ponies up to cover the payroll or tells its story to potential investors?

BETTER TOGETHER

It's well understood that society reveres the individual. From the victorious Celebrity Apprentice to the superstar hockey player, it's the singular character that's most often celebrated on the public stage. But the reality is that most of the world's finest moments have been the results of concerted *group* industry. The Great Pyramids, after all, weren't thrown together by a single guy with a passion for engineering. There was a data-based plan, and there were key roles identified within it, and the plan was followed. Centuries later, the end result still stands.

Collective effort, then, in the form of high-performing corporate teams, always trumps whatever the individual can come up with. And while that reality is undoubtedly a function of how effectively a group is guided by its leader, it's also very much about how motivated its members are — or how good they are at following others. The reward is that great teams are remembered decades later. Think about the best team you every played on or worked with. I can still vividly remember what the Microsoft president Frank Clegg and his GE recruit, Frank Vella, built while I was employed there in the Microsoft heyday time period of the 1990s. It entered the business enterprise space and battled IBM with 90 percent less staff and a whack of passion. We had the right people in the right roles at the right time for the business. And, even better, we had the execution. Frank Clegg impowered Vella to build a team of tenacious, independent leaders with a sense of urgency to capture the banking market for Microsoft as it wanted to enter the enterprise space.

From the start, humans have relied on other humans for survival and success. Depending on how far back one wants to excavate, it's surely the efforts of our parents and our community's top-performing hunters and gatherers that have sustained us. But imagine how much less progress the lot of us would make if we resisted their efforts? Our success is dependent upon our ability to work as a group, implicit in which is the ability of each individual to shuffle off his need to lead and follow effectively.

Teams are human beings' natural working unit. By coming together en masse, we, at the least, survive; at the best, thrive. There's no arguing that high-functioning teams can achieve more than ponderous individuals. Working in tandem means more hands at the wheel, more brains to the challenge. Companies with excellent records of team-driven activity have a powerful edge over their less united competitors.

Current philosophies insist that we draw a distinction between a team and a group. Where a group is a population of individuals who are working toward individual goals, a team is a collective with a common objective. And the best teams are those synergy-burning gatherings whose mutual efforts actually combine to produce performance levels that exceed those of even its strongest members.

BUILDING SMARTER TEAMS

Putting together a team with potential is one thing; ensuring it performs to its fullest capacity is another. That fact is thanks to a misunderstanding of the true and specific potential of a team's members. Only with the benefit of a full psychological report of each individual's profile, including particular mention of those situations in which he or she shines and stumbles, can a team prosper. With such detail, a team can match precisely its own collective of personalities with the functional requirements of each role within it. Anything less ignores the critical reality of your particular mix and fails to appreciate the ways in which its component parts fit together.

It stands to follow that each of us is drawn to a certain occupation according to our personalities. Those practical requirements a particular professional function makes of us should, in a perfect world, align with the talents and preferences we possess in greatest quantity. If we're slow off the mark, for example, and tend to gather speed the further into a task we are, we'd be best placed in a role that doesn't call for rapid-fire action. If we shy from the spotlight, a behind-the-scenes job would be preferable. If we like to be busy and perform best under pressure, a job that frontloads with responsibility and keeps the pedal to the metal would be ideal. What if we're particularly pragmatic? Innovative? Competitive? Results-oriented? Sociable? There are postings that will take advantage of these qualities, too.

PUTTING TEAMS TO THE TEST

Our personalities are largely a result of our earliest days. Scientists conclude that, their occasional exposure to profoundly life-changing experiences notwithstanding, people's overarching character traits become permanent fixtures as we enter adulthood. Given the immovable-force quality of our dispositions, then, it behooves the lot of us to make happy marriages of these innate and inflexible realities with the less locked-in requisites of our jobs.

More than that, though, it's appropriate for us to apply the same rigid standards to our subordinate selves. Leaders need to understand not just those qualities that make them excellent leaders, but also those qualities that allow them to flourish in the *following* role.

We're each of us blessed and cursed with a particular set of strengths and weaknesses. And so it stands to reason that certain personalities will naturally nudge their ways to the command-assuming top. And others will gravitate to the ground. Both things are good. Better still is an appreciation for *why*.

While the world has long understood the value of per-sonality tests in recruiting staffers (namely, for their ability to identify winners from a sea of losers), they are too often overlooked after the fact. But validated personality tests (not the ones that should not and cannot be used legally for hiring) have much to offer organizations in the intelligent and ongoing application of their talent.

By understanding the strengths and weaknesses of every player who's already got a uniform on his back, we can adapt his professional role such that it maximizes the best stuff and minimizes the worst. Recognizing situations in which an employee is most likely to rise to the challenge, and those in which he's most likely to shrink from the scene, will produce a succinctly organized workforce that uses every part of the talent assets.

To perform at their greatest potential, teams need to maintain a thorough mix of psychological roles. These roles must be balanced in terms of both the team member's aptitude for the job at hand, and for his aptitude for working well with others.

By knowing their balance of psychological roles, teams and their managers can identify and correct for performance gaps. In this way, self-awareness is a powerful tool, for teams and individuals both. When a team fails, it's often because its members don't gel and turnovers can explode. But when a team nails it, it has enough diversity within its membership to cover every psychological demand and so can sidestep problems like excessive internal competition, an absence of the self-discipline required to see tasks through, or such hard-driving push for results that customers' satisfaction tends to be overlooked.

TALK ABOUT IT

As with so many scenarios whose chance for success hinges on their superiors' management approach, leaders as followers do best when transparency rules. By being honest with themselves about their value as followers, these people gain precious insight into their value as leaders. By being clear about how they're received by their subordinates, they learn lessons about themselves that they can apply when they reassume the top spot. As bosses, do we prefer to be respected or feared? As employees, do we like to be checked in on or left to our own devices? Both will inform our on-the-job choices.

In any event, no team can be effective if both sides of the equation don't communicate with each other — early and often. Followers perform best if they know what's expected of them. Leaders perform best if they've got enthusiastic buy-in from their followers.

So it's on you to remember the importance of keeping the communication channels wide and open, whether you're having a leading or following day. Otherwise, followers might not understand the mission. They can feel undervalued, and resentment can build. And, depending on the hat you're wearing that day, you might be one of them.

5

How to Decide

DID YOU EVER HAVE TO MAKE UP YOUR MIND? Pick up on one and leave the other behind? Making decisions is an inalienable part of everyone's existence. From what we'll put on our backs in the morning to what we'll put on our TV screens at night, daily life is fraught with the imperative to negotiate choice. And if you're heading up a professional organization upon whose continued existence other people's livelihoods rest (to say nothing of your own), then you're more fraught with the stuff than most.

Every decision involves picking between maintaining the status quo and inviting change. Those can be hefty and wildly disparate options. Landing on the best decision is a significant achievement deserving of considerable celebration. Of course, these celebrations can be precarious things, dependent as they are on an obvious and irrefutable victor — a rare concept in this game, particularly when the stakes are high. No wonder decision-making is considered such a critical leadership skill.

And one worth mastering. If you can learn how to make timely, thoughtful, clever decisions, then you can lead your people to a successful place. But if you can't nail the trick, you risk sinking like a stone and taking your entire team down with you.

TIMING IS EVERYTHING

Every decision has a deadline tied into it. It might be some distance in the future — but it probably isn't. Indeed, one of the most challenging aspects of decision-making is the hovering time frame dictating its dimensions. The need to weigh your options before making a commitment is a real one, but ponder too long and risk analysis paralysis. An old translation of Goethe's *Faust* sums it up thus: "Indecision brings its own delays, and days are lost lamenting over lost days."

There's lots of advice floating around about how to manage the ticking clock that monitors decisiveness. Sometimes, lingering till the last moment is a strategic tack that plunges the other guy into a pressure cooker that makes him blink first. But it can work in the other direction, too, with a luxuriously claimed timeline depriving its presumptuous consumer of the upper hand. Professional athletes — or at least the unions that represent them — know all too well the delicacy with which the timing of a negotiation must be handled. Too many strikes have been the result of one side or the other dragging their arrogant skate blades a little too long and ultimately prompting punitive responses borne of frustration.

FACING THE UNKNOWNS

"Life is the sum of all your choices," Albert Camus once declared. That's heavy stuff that really ups the ante when it comes to the picks you make. Implicit in the prickly business is the powerful role that blind fear has to play in it. Often, it's the looming specter of the *unknown* that's the most unnerving aspect of making a decision. Pick Option A and wonder forever what Option B might have delivered.

Economists call the phenomenon "opportunity cost." In other words, when we elect one course of action, we rule out the others. These cast-off alternatives represent the opportunity cost of any decision. If these costs are too dear for a person to relinquish with a commitment (you know these folks: the ones who've been laboring over whether to quit a job or move house *forever*), she risks becoming an opportunity miser, pathologically immobilized by indecision.

Because it's a brutal fact of life that we simply *can't* know in advance what the consequences of our decisions will be. It's ultimately impossible to rationally calculate opportunity costs, because life is unpredictable. As such, decision-making is a constant gamble. And coming to terms with that big, hairy truth is all part of the adventure.

Psychologists are no strangers to this human preoccupation. Indeed, a huge swath of the shrink-employing population enlists such professional assistance to come to terms with exactly that: the what-ifs that haunt them. The counsel here is straightforward: make a choice and commit to it utterly. If you live in the present with an eye to the future, there's no room for contemplative meanderings on how the thing *might have gone* if only you'd chosen differently.

BRAIN SCIENCE'S DECISION-MAKING PLAY

What role does instinct have to play in making decisions? Any at all? Or should we rely on verifiable evidence alone? Does head always trump gut?

Certainly, the conviction is that mindful, measured calculation of every alternative is the established standard when it comes to the science of determination. In a 2011 *Psychology Today* article on the subject, Gary Klein, a senior scientist at the American research and consulting firm Macro Cognition, said he had no time for gut when it comes to reaching consensus. Conscious and deliberate evaluation is mandatory to the exercise, he argues; anything else is simply too flighty.

But a wealth of new research on *how humans decide* has unearthed surprising revelations, some of which seem to contradict such conventional beliefs.

The unconscious, it turns out, has got a whole lot to say in how we process choice. Indeed, neuroscientists have learned that our brain waves actually predict the outcome of a decision a full 10 seconds before we're able to verbalize it, or even understand that we've arrived at it. This team of researchers from the Max Planck Institute for Human Cognitive and Brain Sciences worked with the Charité University Hospital and the Bernstein Center for Computational Neuroscience (the former in Leipzig, the latter two in Berlin) to study what the internal workings of the human brain look like when confronted with choice. They found that those unconscious areas that handle automatic processes are actually where most decisions are made. The brain considers the information at hand in these under-the-radar corridors, explores the likely consequence of every possibility, and commands an action that aligns with one of them — all without our conscious participation.

Assuming that we're all very *consciously* in control of the choices we make is an arrogant assumption, say the scientists, who speculate that the opposite might occur as a protective measure to keep our brains from becoming congested with the plethora of routine decision-requiring tasks that dominate so much of life.

"We readily accept that most behavior is driven by mental events that we have no access to," Loran Nordgren, an associate professor of management and organizations at the Kellogg School of Management, told a journalist in 2009. "Our heart beats, we pick up a cup or type on a keyboard—all are complicated tasks, but we have no idea how they happen. They take place in a black box; we have no access to it." Do you really need to think about whether to brake at a stop sign or put your socks on under your shoes?

But the folly is in imagining that these unconscious processes stop at basic behavior and don't extend into complex, higher-order concerns. While the question of whether to end a relationship or take a particular job has conventionally been considered the business of the conscious mind, it isn't necessarily so. "It doesn't need to be a pure dichotomy," Nordgren says. "But dominant thinking hasn't been open to this idea."

INSTINCT FAVORS INTRICACY

What's more, the validity of gut deliberation as an approach to choice seems to increase in accordance with the complexity of the decision. The deal, argues a cadre of Dutch researchers in a recent *Science* article, is this: solid, smart decisions draw on a person's cognitive resources. The more complex the decision, the deeper it draws. As such, said resources become depleted in direct relation to the difficulty of the problem, and are rendered increasingly less useful for solving the problem at hand. Intuitive decisions, however, make no such demands on cognition, so the quality of the choice at hand suffers no down-graded influences in conjunction with its complicatedness. The "seemingly counter-intuitive conclusion," goes the article, is that "although simple decisions are enhanced by conscious thought, the opposite holds true for complex thinking."

Daniel Kahneman, a Nobel Prize laureate in economics, agrees that intuition is an important influencer when it comes to making a pick. But he urges caution. Give too much power to the authority of your instinct and risk wrongheaded selection. With today's front-line leaders on average spending 3.5 hours each day influencing others into action, instinct needs a companion tool. This is where workforce analytics enter.

And we should be similarly skeptical of others' instincts. We must exercise wariness when it comes to the stock we put in others' so-called expertise, Kahneman explains in *Psychology Today*. To illustrate, he offers the example of a surgeon and the advice this professional might have to provide on an important decision. The opinion of any individual shouldn't warrant a reflexive accord until he's actually earned the reputation as a voice to be trusted. And that's largely a function of the depth of his experience with similar situations.

In any event, the unconscious approach to decision-making seems a fairly sound one, say those who've tracked after-the-fact outcomes. The journal *Emotion* published a study in which subjects were presented with a series of complex decisions and instructed to either go with their gut or reason it out. Overall, the former was shown to produce the most favorable results.

And so leaders must include both rational, logical thinking *and* unconscious, intuitive thinking in their decision-making pursuits. It could be that there's a sweet spot between logic and emotion that lives in all of us when it comes to the best place from which to make decisions.

———

DECISION-MAKING, DECONSTRUCTED

The process of making a decision is a matter at the serious mercy of a multitude of game-changing factors. From the gender of the person engaged in the exercise and the powers of his own willpower, to the quantity and quality of the data at hand, every decision is subject to a whack of potential outcome benders. In his book, *Willpower: Rediscovering the Greatest Human Strength*, Roy Baumeister, a social psychologist from Florida State University, submits that willpower has a powerful force to exert when it comes to negotiating choice. The people who have enjoyed the most success in their lives, Baumeister believes, are those who have cultivated habits to compensate for deficiencies in their own self-control. Rather than endure excessive stress, these folks have mastered swift decisiveness simply to save themselves from getting mired in uncomfortable crisis.

This touches on the psychological theory of "ego depletion," which contends that we only have a finite supply of self-control and that burning through our reserves on other things leaves less to expend on decision-making. Indeed, there's so much information constantly bombarding our psyches that there's reason to believe that its abundance is a detriment, and not a service. In *The Art of Choosing*, Columbia University professor Sheena Iyengar proposes that today's flood of e-information has the power to overload our cognitive functions. In response to the results of a study she conducted to understand the impact of providing more data to people making investment decisions, she argued that our stated preferences for ever-more statistics, facts, and proofs notwithstanding, excessive information can be "debilitating."

The timing of the arrival of the data that inform our decisions is also a factor. George Loewenstein, a professor of economics and psychology at Carnegie Mellon University in Pittsburgh, says the world puts too much credence in the currency of information. It's easy, he warns, to confuse immediacy for value when it comes to making a choice.

We're also quick to assign value to great volumes of information, as if its sheer magnitude confers on it all kinds of worth. Research conducted by the Center for Neural Decision-Making at Temple University in Philadelphia discovered that when our decision-making facilities are overextended, rational and logical prefrontal cortex functioning declines. In turn, people make lousy decisions and careless mistakes. With too much information, the experiment concluded, our decisions make less and less sense.

That sleep deprivation has a big stick to wield in this game shouldn't be surprising. A lack of sleep, says a National University of Singapore neuroscientist, actually infuses the decision maker with optimism — potentially worrying news for the patients of overextended surgeons.

Finally, a wealth of seemingly trivial things has also been demonstrated to exert authority on the way we make up our minds. If you're hungry, sexually aroused, or in need of a trip to the loo, will it have an impact on the choice you make? Maybe, say a bundle of academic studies exploring the effect of various external factors on a person's decision-making powers. A full bladder, for example, enhances rational thinking. (A Dutch researcher tested the decision-making abilities of two groups; the one that had consumed great quantities of water made better choices.) Same thing with a full stomach: one study by Israeli scientists found that judges were much more likely to grant a convict parole after lunch than at the end of a long day.

And being in a state of sexual arousal during the decision-making process is a biggie (surprise, surprise). Such conditions — predictably — tend to make a person more impetuous. Worse, they blind the subject to exactly how much influence his libido is inflicting. That, says Dan Ariely, a professor of psychology and behavioral economics at Duke University in North Carolina, is because we have but a limited store of emotion and cognition upon which to draw, and depleting one side of the ledger has a meaningful impact on the other.

Even the props and furniture in the scene of one's decision-making exertions have a role to play. One experiment found that people accord more authority to a guy wielding a heavy clipboard than a light one. Another discovered that car shoppers sitting on hard chairs in the dealership will bargain more aggressively than the more comfortably seated petitioner. And if you're holding a hot drink when you meet someone new, says another bit of esoterica, you'll be more open to befriending them than if you're clutching a cold one.

Who knew?

EVIDENCE BEATS OPINION

The presence of evidence to support an argument is a sweet blessing to a person on the horns of a dilemma. With evidence to back you up, a whole heap of decisions is rendered easier to tackle. An evidence-based analytical approach to decisions serves as a radar detector — it enables you to see inside your organization to calculate the pace of change, and to diagnose with great precision both the sources of business value creation and what will slow change down.

DECISION-MAKING TACTICS

All of us make decisions every single day — including many of which we're not even aware. Still, the world has yet to produce a foolproof formula for tackling decisions. Most prevailing prescriptions for doing so urge common sense above all. A few of the more popular strategies in this arena include:

- Deep breathing, to clear your mind for battle.

- Researching, to feel confident that you've got all the information in front of you.

- Listing your options, in either verbal or written form, to keep the whole picture front of mind.

- Following through on the possible outcomes, complete with likely predictions and acknowledgement of whether they're negative or positive (or design yourself a decision tree, that lays out every possible consequence visually).

- Testing your intuition, by imagining a committed decision and then gauging the corresponding feeling it inspires in your gut.

- Taking the time you need, so long as it doesn't become an overly indulgent distraction.

- Evaluating your decision, an after-the-fact exercise that engages a conscious inventory of the lessons learned.

- Coming to terms with your pick, always cognizant of the reality that no decision is going to lead to a perfectly ideal outcome, and that being at peace with your choice is worth lots.

MAKING A DECISION WITH EVERY TOOL ENGAGED

All previous theories on the subject aside, decision-making is both a cognitive *and* an emotional process. Great strategists understand that it's necessary to trust both your intellect *and* your instinct. The relief and peace that come with finally landing on an active verdict are unequalled in the realm of human emotion, and successful business leaders understand this implicitly.

Nobody promised that the decisions you would have to make over the course of your life would be easy. But a conscious appreciation for that reality, and a thoughtful approach to the trickier ones that litter your path, is the smartest bet. The guy who knows that decisions are complex, demanding beasts is surely better prepared to tackle them than the guy who's freshly surprised with each new confrontation by what devils they can be.

DECISION BY JOB INTERVIEW: INSUFFICIENT

It's a hackneyed declaration that's lost its original punch to say that you can't teach natural talent, only skills and knowledge — but that doesn't make it any less accurate. Great managers get this and stack their decks with as much talent as they can. But the *best* managers take the scene a step further and work hard to understand precisely *what* talent they have. Only by gaining a handle on the specific peaks and valleys of the talent landscape at his place of work can a leader organize a professional topography that takes best advantage of those assets.

True enough, one might say. And that's where the job interview comes in. Not so. The serious limitations of the standard job interview are well-known today, with a stack of studies pointing out that these conventional encounters favor candidates who are attractive, socially at ease, articulate, and (curiously) tall. And everyone knows those people who can put on a sweet show for an interview that belies an entirely different reality.

The time commitment required of an interview diminishes its effectiveness further, especially given an employment climate that's sending legions of applicants in pursuit of every last job opening. It's simply too inefficient to conduct an interview with every halfway promising one.

Still, with alarming frequency, managers choose a course for building their teams that's predicated on the arrogant assumption that their takeaway from a 40-minute meeting with a wannabe employee is enough to accurately inform them of their abilities — both on the job and as a member of a high-performing team. Insanity.

Better, by far, would be an approach that seeks to understand, first, what success looks like for you and, next, to nominate the in-house skills and talents that would produce such success. From there, the specific gifts each individual brings to the table can be matched against this identified list, and triumph will be the happy result.

A good first start is to measure mental ability. Without question, the amount of buzz taking place inside an individual's grey matter is going to provide some serious clues as to whether she's a good bet to welcome into your fold. A standard IQ test might do the trick here. But such a test primarily measures a person's mathematical and spatial reasoning, logical ability, and language understanding without accounting for his ability to comprehend, understand, or profit from experience. This measure can then be paired up with a job interview, and the combination will produce an enhanced picture of the person on the block — much more comprehensive than a gut-feel tactic any day.

WHY COGNITION MATTERS

Better still? A test that measures a person's cognition.

Distinct from IQ, cognition is a measure of how we comprehend the world and conduct ourselves within it. It is related to learning, adjusting, understanding, problem-solving, and processing complex information. Cognitive abilities are the brain-based skills we need to carry out any task — from the simplest to the most tangled. This gauge is more akin to the mechanisms of how we learn, remember, solve problems, and pay attention than it is to any actual knowledge.

Since the publication of Charles Spearman's influential writings on intelligence in the early part of the last century, science has universally accepted that a unitary factor of cognitive ability (or intelligence) exists: the so-called g factor. In our experience with clients, the need to get a "second flashlight" on people they hire, promote, or train has become an added people advantage. The NFL has used cognitive surveys to measure all potential players they draft for years. Our tool of choice at Predictive Success is called the Professional Learning Indicator® (PLI®), see http://pli-canada.com. Its dynamic nature gives it an edge in the cognitive test marketplace. It is an innovative cognitive test loaded up with g-factor content that, in 12 minutes, measures an individual's general cognitive ability by way of 50 multiple-choice questions. The assessment is made up of inquiries from three areas key to success within organizations: numeric, verbal, and abstract reasoning. It's a dynamic survey, where the questions change every time you take it, making it highly individualized and suitable for employees on all levels. The test provides valuable quantifiable information about someone's ability to learn, adjust, understand, solve problems, and process complex information.

A person's cognitive ability correlates with his potential for performance acceleration inside a professional role. Whether she is an individual contributor or the CEO, someone's benchmark PLI® score can help identify those candidates who are most likely to succeed in a given position. Regardless of level within an organization, folks whose scores put them within the upper tier of a given data range will have a greater chance of exceeding expectations for that position than anyone else.

PLI®: FOR MORE THAN HIRING

Education is vital for employee development. The PLI® tells a supervisor the employee's path to learning. It could be a quick jaunt to new knowledge or an extended ordeal. The latter could be ideal for an academic role but absolutely not helpful for a role in direct sales. To get the most out of the PLI®, managers need to test all employees. This can provide valuable benchmarking data to identify preferred scores for a specific position. Over time, organizations using the PLI® enjoy the advantage of being able to analyze how individuals with disparate backgrounds coexist. And succession planning gets a boost with the PLI® for the powers it lends an organization to groom leaders internally from junior positions on up. From our experience with leading companies, some employees have a shorter "take off to learning" than others. For example, some employees need a much longer runway to gain new knowledge. If this information is made available to the frontline supervisor, the onboarding experience is made dramatically better. We have seen companies reduce onboarding time by as much as 50 percent with the PLI® along with the Predictive Index.

The need to identify "next gen" high-potential talent is urgent in companies today. When companies bring in objective data like the PLI®, they increase the level of "fairness" in the entire high potential program and also "amp up" the diversity in their people choices.

6

How to Persuade

HOW COME CERTAIN PEOPLE SEEM SO UNCOMMONLY blessed when it comes to their ability to win others over to their point of view? Exactly what is it about some individuals that they possess an uncanny ability to nudge the sentiments of others into their favor, even if they launch the process at opposite ends of the spectrum of opinion?

Mastering this important skill should be a life lesson each and every one of us takes on. The ability to persuade other people about something is a critical one that finds constant application throughout a person's life, in a multitude of personal, social, and professional situations. You may want to persuade an employee to smarten up or deliver more. You may want to persuade your boss to give you a raise or adopt your idea. And if you're a kid—the most pervasive persuaders of us all—you probably want to persuade your parents of almost everything.

In any event, understanding the trick to persuasion will deliver certain happiness and satisfaction to your life, as opposed to a perpetual state of dissatisfaction and frustration. If you can persuade people, you can achieve your goals, both big and small. More than that, cultivating an appreciation for the techniques of persuasion will heighten your sensitivity to those occasions when they're being wheeled out on you. That'll keep more money in your pocket and won't fill your closets up with infomercial-peddled junk, if nothing else.

THE ROLE OF THE SUBCONSCIOUS

The more sensitive you are to the subtleties of persuasion, the more likely you'll be able to use them in your own attempts to persuade. That means digging below the purely superficial strategies — such as laying out a clear verbal case for your argument and directing someone's attention to the patently obvious benefits to be gained by signing on with you (though the value of these should not be diminished) — and exploiting the constant participation of the subconscious in humans' decision-making process.

Here, you dip into advertisers' bags of tricks, long a trove of ploys aimed at swaying the public's subliminal response mechanisms in a particular direction. That means, for example, taking care to frame your pitch in such a way that it influences your intended target's reception of the same in a positive way. So if the glass is presented as half full, instead of half empty, well, that's going to be a more desirable proposition than the other. In this way, persuaders can have a hand in shaping the meaning and associations another person attaches to something.

These framing tools find play in carefully chosen, emotionally-charged language that conjures up affirmative, encouraging internal images and feelings about otherwise objective ideas or things. A clever politician understands that his stance on the controversial issue of abortion comes cloaked in more positive associations if he describes it by way of a "pro" way in. "*Pro*-life" and "*pro*-choice" simply leave a better taste in the mouth than "*anti*" anything. Always consider the subtle distinctions in the language you choose in making your case, and land on those words that'll leave the other guy with a bright, comfortable impression in his gut.

SPEAKING FROM THE CORPS

The subconscious also kicks into gear in the physicality a person employs in his efforts to persuade. The body language you adopt when you're standing in another person's view while you work to convince him of your point is key in winning him to your side. If you're closed up physically, you look shifty, and people will be apt to suspect you're not sharing the whole truth. If you present a physical openness, though, others will feel you're coming clean with them, and will be more likely to believe your words.

Your body can also be engaged in your persuasive gambit if you use it to mirror the physicality of the person you're trying to convert. If you mimic his body language and movements, you automatically establish a sense of empathy. Move in when he moves in, cock your head when he does, talk emphatically with your hands when he does, too. Take care to be subtle and judicious here (lest the other guy suspect that you're a loon), and you'll be rewarded with a simpatico milieu that's conducive to communion.

EMULATING EMO

Another area in which the subconscious can be used to your advantage is in an appreciation of the emotional state of your intended target. Here, something along the opposite lines of the lesson parents learn early, about not asking demanding things of their toddler when he's tired or hungry, applies. In this case, it's actually *more* likely that someone who's feeling a bit mentally fatigued will bend to your cause. It's been proven, in fact, that people are more agreeable and submissive when they're emotionally worn down. Rather than struggle with yet another taxing decision, they would sooner acquiesce and sign on the dotted line. Use that reality to your advantage by approaching your targets at the end of a long workday, say, or after they've just played a punishing game of squash.

Another timing-related ploy that the subconscious can make subtle use of is to jump to a conclusion before you've actually landed there. The driver who waves his thanks to a fellow motorist who's unwittingly let him in feels obliged to make good on the assumption, and so lets his car squeeze ahead of her. The salesman who enthusiastically shakes his mark's hand while the negotiation is still ongoing looks to secure the certainty of an outcome before it's been reached. In this way, you've achieved a key point in your objective's favor: you've managed to get the other person behaving in a way that suggests a decision has been reached—before it has.

Other techniques designed to subconsciously persuade another to your way of thinking include:

- The use of so-called fluent speech that sidesteps common conversation breakers like "um" that, while practically allowing a person to collect his thoughts, actually serve to diminish the sought-after impression that he's confident and in control.

- Working your magic in the company of a dog. By having a pooch by your side while you're talking, you automatically bestow a comfort level to the scene, to say nothing of a sense that you're a compassionate, loyal person, which can only work to your benefit. If you don't have a dog, borrow one, and, if that's not possible, put pictures of dogs up on your desk.

- Offering your target of persuasion coffee. There is something about cradling a hot beverage in your hands while listening to a proposition that can instill receptive feelings of warmth in a person.

- Setting the scene by asking affirmative questions. If you launch your conversation with lots of queries that demand "yes" answers, you'll confer a positive energy to the interaction.

- Using touch to get what you want. If you're comfortable with this, and if the situation can appropriately sustain such a thing, it's useful to occasionally lay a convivial hand on his person.

THE STANFORD PRISON EXPERIMENT

In 1971, a team of psychology researchers from Stanford University set out to understand the dimensions of humans' ability to be persuaded. The Stanford Prison Experiment (SPE) asked a group of volunteers to submit to an unusual set of social conditions so their actions might demonstrate just how powerful one person's influence could be over another.

In it, 24 male students were assigned a role as either a prisoner or a guard in a mock prison that was set up in the basement of the university's psychology building. Led by psychology professor Philip Zimbardo, the 12 "prisoners" and 12 "guards," selected for their criminal-free backgrounds and demonstrated psychological health, were instructed that they would be subjected to a mock prison environment for between seven and 14 days (for which they would be paid $15 a day). The guards were told that their objective was to create a situation of powerlessness for the prisoners. They were not to physically harm them, though they could impose situations that inspired boredom and a certain amount of fear. The guards were given batons to establish their authority, and the prisoners were assigned numbers and had chains attached to their ankles.

The experiment deteriorated quickly. Several guards abused their power, denying prisoners basic rights, like their mattresses, clothes, and the ability to use the toilet, and ultimately subjecting them to physical and psychological torture. For their part, many of the prisoners accepted this abuse passively, some even harassing other prisoners who attempted to thwart it. The experiment, certain parts of which were filmed for public consumption, was terminated after six days.

The experiment is notable to this day for its demonstration of how impressionable people are when furnished with a legitimizing ideology and social and institutional support. Both guards and prisoners embraced their assigned roles fully. And, in spite of a hypothesis that prisoners' and guards' inherent personality traits are the chief cause of abusive behavior in prison, the research revealed that it's the persuasive powers of a situation, in fact, that compel a person to act in a certain way, and not their prevailing personalities.

ASKING FOR MORE

As absurd as it sounds, sometimes the best way to get what you want is to ask for even more. This, possibly the most ironic of a rich assortment of proven persuasion tactics, advises the person looking to convince someone else of something to dive deep with his request from the start. Consider: if you want the other guy to donate $10 to your charitable campaign, ask him for $25. In this way, you establish an implied precedent that suggests that $25 is what everyone else is giving. Suddenly, even though $10 is your ultimate target, you've set up a scene that shrewdly shames the guy with a false impression. So he refuses the $25 give, but concedes, after all, to $10. And you've won.

In this way, you've persuaded by setting up a pressure-laden situation that you subsequently open the valve on. Both of you look like heroes, with you making a charitable concession and the other person feeling the satisfaction of having their lesser gift accepted after all.

The power of this persuasion method draws on the other person's sense of obligation to reciprocate the allowance you so generously made. People tend to be more receptive to grant your actual (albeit lesser) request after they've declined the first (and bigger) one. Indeed, they'll feel embarrassed to also turn down the second favor, especially if it's set up to appear much easier to oblige than the first.

More than that, your second request gives them the gift of freedom of choice. With it, you've provided them both an escape route and the distinction of granting a special favor. By indulging this second demand, your nego-tiating partner will feel a sense of contentment and, at the same time, a sense of responsibility to fulfill the secondary (and even other future) requests. What comes into critical play with this approach is the sense of guilt someone feels when they refuse someone else's request. If your subsequent appeal is for something they can afford to accommodate, they'll leap at the chance to make their initial disappointment up to you.

This emerges as one of the most potent persuasion tech-niques because it affords the other guy the opportunity to negotiate — a powerful psychological booster — while simultaneously making her feel that she got the better end of the deal because you reduced your original request.

THE *FORBES* LIST

After studying the behavior of some of the world's most influential political, social, business, and religious leaders, *Forbes* magazine recently published 21 "critical lessons" it identified as being meaningful to successful persuasion.

They, along with a brief explanation of each, are paraphrased below:

1. **Distinguish persuasion from manipulation**. Manipulation is coercion through force to get someone to do something that's not in her own interest. Persuasion, on the other hand, is the art of getting people to do things that are in their best interest, but that will also benefit you. When you are equipped with great insight on the other person's core drives and motivations, you are "advantaged." From my experience, tools like the Predictive Index® and Professional Learning Indicator® give you this information.

2. **Persuade the persuadable**. Everyone (given the right timing and context) can be persuaded, goes this school of thought, but not necessarily in the short term. It's this conviction that sees political campaigns focusing their resources on a relatively small set of voters whose swing status ultimately decides elections. And so it is that the first step of persuasion has to be identifying those people that, at a given time, are amenable to being nudged to

your point of view and focusing your energy and attention on them.

3. **Remember the value of context and timing**. These are the basic building blocks of persuasion. Context creates a relative standard of what's possible. And timing offers a freeze-frame window into what we want at a given point in our lives. We choose to marry a different type of person from the one we choose to date, for example, because what we want when we're younger is different from what we want when we're older.

4. **You have to be interested to be persuaded.** You can't persuade someone to do something or behave in a certain way if he's simply not interested. And the top of the "interests list" for all of us is ourselves. So if you can focus your persuasive efforts on the other guy, you'll probably get the all-important foot in the door. After that, remember that we spend most of our time thinking about love, money, and health, so bear these topics in mind in your subsequent conversational maneuvers, and you should be good to go.

5. **Reciprocity compels**. When somebody does something for someone else, a ledger is automatically created that keeps a running tally of debts owed. We either create "trust deposits or trust withdrawals." So if I treat you well, you're going to subconsciously be aware of an imbalance in our relationship that you'll feel compelled to address. You can use this powerful debt meter to your advantage by showering small gestures of consideration on others and standing by for their reflexive payback impulse to kick in.

6. **Persistence pays**. The person who's willing to keep asking for what he wants, and who continues to

offer a demonstrable value behind his requests, is ultimately the most persuasive. There are a slew of historical examples featuring doggedly persistent characters whose names we remember for winning their objectives just by nothing more than sheer and dogged tenacity.

7. **Compliment sincerely**. It's not rocket science to accept that humans are more well-disposed to people who treat them warmly than they are to people who do not. So compliment people about aspects of their personality or actions that you genuinely believe to be worthy of praise. Be creative, and applaud those features about them for which they probably aren't typically complimented. It's a remarkably easy thing you can do to persuade others, and it doesn't cost you a thing.

8. **Set expectations**. Much of persuasion is tied up in your ability to successfully manage other people's expectations as they relate to trusting in your judgment. The CEO who promises a 20 percent increase in sales and supplies 30 percent is going to set up some positive associations with his ability to deliver, while the same CEO who promises a 40 percent boost but produces only 35 percent will suffer an entirely different reputation. Persuasion is simply about understanding and over delivering on other's expectations.

9. **Don't assume**. It is unwise to assume what someone needs, and it is better, always, to explore the specifics. In sales we'll often hold back from offering our products/services because we assume others don't have the money or interest. Better to be clear on what you can provide and leave the choice to them.

10. **Create a condition of scarcity**. Almost everything has value on a relative scale. In other words, we want something because everyone else wants it, too. So if you're angling to have someone feel desirous of something (or someone), withhold that thing. Its relative value will increase in turn.

11. **Create a condition of urgency**. If you're keen to have your target of persuasion act swiftly, you need to set down conditions that'll motivate her to do so. We have to persuade people in the present, and urgency is the most valuable card we have to play.

12. **Images matter**. What we see, science has revealed, carries more weight than what we hear. Skeptical? Consider those drug commercials that rattle off a laundry list of utterly unpleasant possible side effects on top of a string of visuals of loving couples playing in the surf or running through fields with their dogs. Ideally, you'll hone your ability to paint an appealing image of the outcome for this person if he chooses to buy into your offer.

13. **Tell the truth**. As counterintuitive as this may sometimes feel, you should always aim to share the truth with others, even if it's kind of brutal to hear. People respect other people who are willing to cut to the chase and share meaningful, pertinent realities without judgment or agenda, which sycophantic others might be too cowardly to discuss.

14. **Build a rapport**. We like people who we are like. Finding common ground on this front might be as simple and subconscious as mirroring and matching our partner's physical behaviors, language patterns, and body language. Whatever it takes to establish a simpatico environment with another individual,

embrace it. The comfort level you build in his gut for these efforts will pay off with affirmation.

15. **Cultivate behavioral flexibility**. Research has shown that it's the guy who exhibits the most flexibility, and not necessarily the guy with the most power, who is actually in control of a situation. Kids know this and will cycle through a catalogue of behaviors to get what they want. The larger your repertoire of behaviors, the more persuasive you'll be.

16. **Learn to transfer energy**. Some people drain us of our energy, while others infuse us with more. The most persuasive people know how to transfer their energy to others, to motivate and invigorate them. That might be simply making eye contact with someone, or responding actively and enthusiastically to what he's telling you.

17. **Communicate clearly**. Not surprisingly, this is a critical one. It's vital to be able to get your point across succinctly if you have any hopes of having it accepted by the person across the table. Ultimately, successful persuasion is an exercise in simplifying something down to its core and communicating to others what they really care about.

18. **Be prepared**. It's an off-the-bat advantage for your cause if you approach it in a state of utter preparedness. If you've done homework into those things about the other person that are important to him, like the products his company sells or some meaningful details of his personal life, then you've set the scene with an upper hand.

19. **Detach and stay calm in conflict**. In situations of heightened emotion, you'll always enjoy more leverage if you can stay calm, detached, and unemotional.

If you lose your stuff because the situation takes a turn for the dramatic, you also stand to lose the other guy's faith in your ability to see your offer through.

20. **Use anger purposefully**. There's no shame in allowing a flash of anger to creep into your campaign of persuasion—so long as it does so in a measured, sparing, and eminently self-controlled way. Indeed, your passion for your objective, so long as it's kept in reasonable check, can be turned to your advantage here.

21. **Be confident**. There's no quality so compelling, intoxicating, and attractive as certainty. If you project and maintain a poised and assertive sense of confidence throughout your pitch, you will be rewarded with the other person's reflected faith in your convictions. If you really believe in what you do, you will always be able to persuade others to do what's right for them—while also getting what you want along the way.

7

How to Communicate

COMMUNICATION IS THE EXCHANGE OF INFORMATION AND ideas from one individual to another. In its simplest forms, it involves a sender conveying something to a recipient. A manager sticks her head into her sales manager's office and delivers a directive, shoots an e-mail to her executive assistant, or sends a memo to her product development team. Done.

Sounds simple, right? Think again.

Brewing under the surface of this operation is a boatload of potential for trouble. Effective communication, after all, only takes place if the recipient understands the data that the sender intended to transmit. And there are numerous examples of corporate initiatives that failed for no more reason than a stumble in communication.

COMMUNICATION RULES

Though it might not be immediately apparent, managers actually spend the bulk of their days communicating. A 1991 study concluded that conventional communication takes up between 70 and 90 percent of leaders' time every day. Add cellphones, e-mails, texting, and tweeting to the mix and the numbers soar.

The ability to communicate effectively is, arguably, the most important ingredient in a business leader's fortunes. Lots of research singles out excellent communication skills in a review of exactly what it takes to achieve success and be promoted in an organization. Recent studies in communication at MIT looked at linear and rich media communication and found that most extroverts preferred "rich media." This is identified as personal/face-to-face interactions. This group actually needs the confrontation to complete the delivery of their messages. The introverts actually preferred linear, data-driven communication, such as e-mail, notes, and texts. The two camps' approaches are very different.

In his book *Beyond the Hype: Rediscovering the Essence of Management,* Dr. Nitin Nohria, using Aristotelian theory, declared that the world's most effectual leaders are masters of the three classical elements of rhetoric the philosopher identified long ago. "You can reach people through logos or logic, by appealing to their sense of what is rational," Aristotle opined. "You can use pathos, appealing to their emotions; or you can make an argument based on their sense of values or ethos."

Truly great leaders, Nohria believes, know how to employ all three of Aristotle's rhetorical elements. "Communication," he has said, "is the real work of leadership."

Indeed. It's why poor communication is so often cited as a key contributor in the failure of major efforts to effect corporate change. It's also why Bill Black, the former president and CEO of Maritime Life, once called communication "one of the three or four central jobs of the CEO." People, he pointed out, "want the CEO to communicate the strategic issues; the 'big-picture' questions. For things happening at the corporate level, they want to hear it from the top."

That loads up the expectation meter for folks in the big office. But becoming proficient in killer communication is a very achievable goal. Read on.

DO UNTO OTHERS

Ask any comedian: What's the trick to blowing away a crowd? After he makes a joke about timing, he'll level with you. It's having a handle on the people with whom you're attempting to communicate. The best communicators know in their bones that the more intimate and comprehensive an understanding they have of their target audience, the more likely they'll be able to reach them.

Comedians are often seen as great communicators. The best comedians, by the way, would be vision setting; able to technically look at humor and anticipate its impact; have a sense of urgency and be able to plan the joke through execution. On stage, however, they create a new "self-concept" where they consciously work to "sell the joke" and deliver only the level of detail required for execution.

It's all about positioning.

Because just as there are a multitude of different personalities populating the planet, so too there are a multitude of different styles of communicating with them. Some people are partial to an unvarnished and direct approach; others would bristle at such presumption and would prefer a lighter hand. Everybody brings a different context to bear on a situation, and it's wrongheaded in the extreme to imagine that the guy you're talking to has the same historical, cultural, and experiential reference points as you. Identifying your communication strategy — preferred method, level of detail, force of delivery, and so on — and how it can help you to succeed is job one. This is no small task: it requires a 10,000-foot strategy for success.

CASE STUDY: COMMUNICATION AT STANLEY MANUFACTURING, TORONTO, CANADA

Dean Anderson is president and CEO of Stanley Manufacturing Company Inc., a longstanding and diversified graphic communications firm with over 40,000 square feet of manufacturing space between its Toronto and Montreal facilities. Not too long ago, this little operation was wrestling with the all-too-familiar challenge of having the right people in the right positions. With just 35 employees, it was critical that every person be well placed at this almost 100-year-old firm.

So it was that Anderson and his team turned to the Predictive Index® and its powers to improve recruiting decisions. Anderson was blown away. "PI® has really transformed the way we onboard new talent," he crows. "Using it has made it easy to get new hires on board and make sure that they're successful when they get into their role."

More than that, PI® has proven a boon to improving communication channels at a company that once struggled with such things, and also to set the place up — from a human relations perspective — for a time when Anderson is no longer at its helm.

The trick, ultimately, to successfully navigating the sea of personality types out there is to take on an appreciation for this home truth: *it's about more than just you.* In other words, it's on each of us to make an effort to understand the subtleties of the individual communication styles of those with whom we might wish to converse.

So as much as your mother might have pushed the idea that we should do unto others as we would have done unto ourselves, the opposite is actually true: we should do unto others *as we would have done unto them.* Full stop. There are no mirrors in this maxim; only windows.

The required wisdom, here? Marry your natural communication style with that of others with whom you seek communion.

SIMPLICITY ABOVE ALL

No one knows for sure who declared: "If I had more time, I would have written a shorter letter" (the quote's been variously assigned to Voltaire, Hemingway, Proust, and Twain). But whoever it was, they were onto something. Brevity and concise expression are critical for delivering a point. There's simply no place for repetition in the CEO's chair. Leaders need to become experts in the art of efficient, succinct communication.

The trick is to distill a complicated concept into something accessible enough that the average person might actually be able to wrap his mind around it. Shoot too high with your high-flown language and risk losing half the crowd on the ascent. "Speak comfortable words!" William Shakespeare urged. Great leaders understand this in their bones, and so deliver their messages, however complex, inside the confines of a few well-chosen statements.

BODY LANGUAGE SPEAKS VOLUMES

That we communicate via more than just the words that tumble out of our mouths is irrefutable. In our Influencing Focused Skills class at Predictive Success, our managing principals teach not only awareness of personality but also of body language. A legion of studies point to the contributions our nonverbal communication makes to our message. Dr. Albert Mehrabian, a psychology prof from UCLA, was a pioneer of this strategy. Early in his research efforts, he determined the following:

- Just 7 percent of the messages we convey that pertain to feelings or attitudes are expressed with spoken words.

- 38 percent of the messages we convey that pertain to feelings or attitudes are expressed paralinguistically (the nonverbal elements in speech such as the tone of voice, look in the eyes, and prevailing emotional state).

- 55 percent of the messages we convey that pertain to feelings or attitudes are expressed via facial expression.

The flurry of second-by-second internal decisions we make and the body language we employ to convey them are red-flag signals to the world about what we *really* mean to say. To deliver the full impact of a message, leaders must, first, be aware of their nonverbal behaviors and, next, capitalize on them. Everything—from when you blink in the midst of an announcement to whether you enter an employee's office to talk or just linger in the doorway—is subject to scrutiny when you're the guy heading up a team of other people whose very livelihood is dependent upon your choices. Make them wisely, and be ever mindful of the extent of input that nonverbal business plays into them. You're being watched.

COMMUNICATING WITH YOUR EARS

Nobody said communication was a one-way street. As well as a leader might speak, he must listen with twice the aptitude. Because as critical as it is for a member of a company's c-suite to cultivate excellence in conversing and corresponding with his people, that's really only half the job. The follow-up is wrapped tightly in a leader's listening skills. Predictable success follows when we treat others as they want to be treated. We can help any company hire the A players, but it's how they manage them that will ultimately dictate success.

It's more than a clever information nugget to point out that hearing and listening are distinct activities. Hearing is the involuntary act of perceiving sound; listening is an active pursuit that involves not just *receiving* but *interpreting* sound. An audience that's *listening* is the ideal to which leaders should consistently aspire.

People speak at 100 to 175 words per minute, but they can listen intelligently at 600 to 800 words per minute. That leaves a gaping hole through which a truckload of distraction might drift in if the listener isn't engaged in what's being communicated to him. The best listeners are able to control that drift, spend more time listening than talking, keep the focus on the other guy and off themselves, and initiate responses only *after* their conversational partner has finished speaking, not during.

Active, reciprocal communication is the critical link between leaders and their stakeholders. It's madness to leave such important business to chance. As such, it's useful for managers to institute a policy of regular location visits and direct electronic communication with subordinates so they might be privy to their on-the-job experience. Recurring forums during which team members might discuss specifics about what's working for them, and what isn't, allow for the kind of free-flowing exchange of information that characterizes an engaged and motivated workforce. In some thriving companies, staffers are even invited to rate senior managers on their communication skills. Such commentary can be a bitter pill, but its consumption has much to offer.

Taken together, the message managers deliver by establishing formalized channels through which workers might share their thoughts with senior leadership is clear: your opinion matters. And it's meaningful to remember that the efforts leaders make to encourage feedback within their organizations won't go unrewarded. Workers will acknowledge such displays of respect from their superiors with increased commitment and productivity. Attention paid to internal communication compensates at every point along the scale.

BUILDING TRUST THROUGH COMMUNICATION

Trust is a concept that's quite splendid in its simplicity: It's the undisputed belief one person has that another person has his best interests at heart. Leaders of high-performing companies are respected for their policy of open-book communication. Information is shared openly in these environments, and employees and stakeholders feel sufficiently informed. But such scenarios, alas, are not as common as they might be. See Figure 7.1.

A 2003 Towers Perrin study called "Enhancing Corporate Credibility: Is It Time to Take the Spin Out of

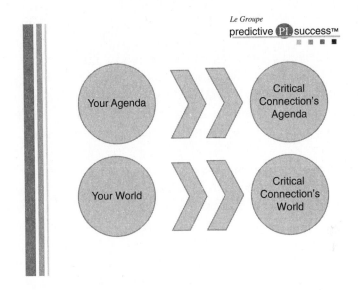

Figure 7.1   Critical Connections

Employee Communications?" concluded that less than half of the 1,000 working Americans it polled consider the corporate communications their employers disclose about their strategy, performance, and competitive challenges to be trustworthy. About a quarter of them came right out and accused the things of being "dishonest."

There's no shortage of precedence in the prickly arena of misspent trust. Thanks to Kenneth Lay, Martha Stewart, and a thousand lesser-known characters whose misdemeanors are catalogued somewhere below the notoriety of these two, the world's suffered its share of abusive leaders who've taken advantage of their subordinates (to say nothing of their investors and customers) and left their faith in tatters.

Not a good foundation from which to operate a business.

Trust is a commanding tool in a leader's gambit to build loyalty and increase credibility in the corporate playground. An organization will face a tough haul in its efforts to motivate, engage, and retain staffers if its leader's messages aren't believed. Simply put, people won't follow a manager in whom they have no faith. And companies can't succeed if their employees aren't in alignment. Once trust is lost, it's tough to get it back. We continue to see the need in our work with leaders for additional data, such as those made available in the Predictive Index®, so they might fully plan their "script" for building and maintaining trust.

Conversely, a workforce whose members have confidence in their leaders and feel satisfied that they've been well apprised of what's happening within the company will be more prolific and more inclined to make contributions designed to spur further progress.

Enter communication, and the powers it has to transform a skeptical population into one that's meaningfully more industrious. An effective manager can use communication to establish a situation in which employees feel secure enough in their position to believe in its continuity and to make contributions from it.

More than that, an environment of trust gives a leader a store of confidence and authority from which to draw in situations where it's essential that he be listened to — and believed. Because trust is particularly important on those occasions when companies hit rough patches or periods of transformation. During uncertain times, transparency drives trust and employee engagement. One leader who has failed to inspire faith in his team might throw them into paroxysms of indecision and despair with a restructuring announcement, say, whereas another, who has taken the time to nurture a culture of integrity and reliability, will be able to draw on that reserve in that time. When your key players feel secure, they're more motivated to perform.

An enduring practice of effective communication is at the heart of the imperative to cultivate a workplace with the essential spirit of confidence in its leadership.

COMMUNICATION TACTICS

While strong leadership is fundamental to business success, an organization can only succeed when its every last employee understands the lay of the land. A leader's grasp of the power of clear, concise, compelling communication is key to such a scene. This essential includes an understanding of what motivates the members of an intended audience to listen — and what motivates them to act.

A manager has a range of opportunities to achieve this. At one end of the spectrum find formalized meetings at which a manager might deliver prepared addresses or make official announcements; at the other, find a myriad of little conversations, from quick-hit verbal exchanges in the hall to full-on bull sessions in the lunchroom.

At a leading North American bank and Predictive Success client, "leadership dialogues" are regularly scheduled meetings at which a senior leader shares stories with an emerging one. These one-on-one sessions are valuable both for the personal touch they bring to the exchange and for the level of commitment a leader demonstrates to his underlings by engaging in this way. At Maritime Life, managers hold regular lunchtime forums with subsets of the staff, gathering just a dozen or so into a congregation whose dimensions are manageable enough for everyone to participate.

Formal or informal, in-person or technologically-facilitated, the key thing is for leaders to ensure that efficient and effective communication is taking place, in some form, in their workplace.

COMMUNICATIONS LEADER, LEAD THYSELF

While the value of conducting an employee survey to gauge the effectiveness of an executive's communication skills is considerable (and the post-survey exercise perhaps even more so), such a thoughtful assessment shouldn't be limited to those on the receiving end of leadership edicts. It's just as useful for professionals in leadership positions to invite others to contribute to regular appraisals of themselves.

The first step to discovering how they are received by others requires managers to cultivate a greater sense of emotional intelligence, or the capacity to understand their own emotions and those of other people. I call this fully understanding your own core DNA or the Predictive Index® for you, the leader. Do a deep dive with all the data and know that the top graph, your "self-graph," will have much to say. The Predictive Index® statistics provide a kind of second picture of you on the job — or the self-concept. Who are you under stress? What's happening to you in your role? Are you in the right role to be successful? What reflexes do you see the need to make? How is your morale? What is your capacity for absorbing all of these changes? Are you congruent? The Predictive Index® program provides you with all of this insight.

For example, my son Curtis has always enjoyed golf. He shot his first hole in one when he was just 11. Impressive. He was able to parlay his golf skills into a golf scholarship in the NCAA Division II Sunshine Conference with Eckerd College in St. Petersburg, Florida. Curtis's Predictive Index® shows he has a lack of patience and a fair degree of assertiveness. As such, whatever his skills as a golfer, when stress takes hold on about day three of many of his tournaments, his lack of patience and appetite for risk-taking have raised his scores and had a negative impact on his finish. When he practices self-awareness on the course, though, his performance improves.

Some questions a leader might reflectively pose on this front:

- Am I communicating *precisely* what I intend to?

- Have I appropriately invited feedback (without pain) from my target audience?

- Have I employed intimidation (even bullying) in my methods?

- Am I leading from my highest PI® factor *and* my lowest?

- Do I have a communication strategy that guides all my communication activities?

- Is my message consistently aligned with my organization's vision and values?

- Have I considered how my employees prefer to receive communication?

- Am I delivering a consistent message to the people I work with each day?

- Am I always the best version of myself when I lead?

As a broker of information and strategy, a leader's ability to appraise his own communication facilities is critical. Only with this kind of self-reflection can he appreciate whether he's being the communication champion he aspires to be. And if a brutally candid valuation thus unearths areas in which a manager might improve, he can call upon help as required. We also know that employees leave the leader, not the company. The bottleneck is the frontline leader. Are your leaders self-aware?

BARRIERS TO COMMUNICATION

Communication is the transmission of information from one person to another. Its apparent simplicity aside, a great number of potential obstructions present a constant threat to its success. Understanding them and the interfering role they have the ability to play in one's broadcast efforts can go a long way to mitigating them. This very long list includes:

- Personal bias ("I am okay; I need people like me");
- Ambient noise;
- Ego;
- An overemphasis on the facts (to the exclusion of the intent);
- Stress (under stress, we all go to our highest *and* lowest PI® factors);
- Environmental distractions (e.g., drama in the team, fire drills).

The only way to overcome these communication busters is to be aware of them. Just as a mother knows to consider whether her child is overtired or hungry in interpreting his cranky cues, a leader needs to take stock of the plethora of influences that are shaping the delivery and receipt of communication initiatives at his business.

COMMUNICATION TIPS

In a 2001 *Harvard Business Review* article, Robert Cialdini argued that "no leader can succeed without mastering the art of persuasion." Influencing well accelerates the growth path for leaders. The ability to have a process to understand others is essential. We have seen dramatic success along these lines with the Influencing Skills Assessment Test (ISAT) from PI Worldwide. (See http://www.pi worldwide.com/solutions/influencing-skills-system.) Here, specific metrics in the five steps a leader needs to effectively communicate with impact are identified. Where is the leader's score in how she opens a meeting? Does she have the ability to set the verbal agenda? Does she investigate well and answer objections linking her capabilities to the client's world? Does she create a natural path to easily having future conversations?

With that in mind, here are some pointers to guide a leader's communication efforts:

- Check in regularly with your audience to ensure that they're following you;
- Provide those on the receiving end of your message with ample opportunity to comment and ask questions;
- Make eye contact with the person with whom you're speaking;
- Vary your tone and pace and keep your conversational partner's Predictive Index® in mind;
- Continue to visit your Predictive Index® Critical Connection Maps;
- Don't ignore signs of confusion in your recipient.

8

How to Assess

IN THE UNITED STATES, MILLIONS OF PEOPLE — 10.5 million in March 2014 — are looking for work. At the same time, a multitude of businesses struggle to operate with incomplete staffs. Vacancies in certain organizations and in certain fields are rampant, because management simply can't find the right candidates to fill the positions. Manpower confirms this with a recent study in which almost half of the 1,361 American employers it polled said they were suffering because they couldn't find staffers with the appropriate skills. This deprives the country of the productivity it needs to compete with emerging powerhouses like China. In his compelling book, *Competing on Analytics: The New Science of Winning*, Thomas H. Davenport writes that mismatched personality is the most frequent cause of productivity drains in North American business.

And so it's not enough to have a populous workforce. It needs to be a workforce whose makeup is an accurate reflection of the needs it purports to serve. But how do we see this through? Exactly how does one calibrate its human assets in the most effective manner? The answer: behavioral assessments.

Because, while qualified expertise in certain technical areas is a part of the puzzle, the kind of data uncovered by behavior analyses and other predictive efforts — data that reveal some of the softer attributes of a workforce's members — are just as important.

Behavior assessments give leaders real information for determining the right button to push. By identifying people's motivations and drives, leaders can put workers in roles that are most suited to them and their core personality — while improving employee retention, developing future leaders, cultivating team performance, and managing talent.

CASE STUDY: THE BIG BROTHERS BIG SISTERS® ORGANIZATION

Big Brothers Big Sisters of Canada® is among the many organizations that have realized the benefits of the Predictive Index®. The CEO of this, one of Canada's most well regarded charities, turned to PI® when he was wrestling with a slew of critical HR issues and was keen to learn how to incorporate big data into professional practice in a way that might address them. Structured like a franchise with 122 local agencies, Big Brothers Big Sisters of Canada® sports a far-flung duty roster whose members were neither well employed in their positions, nor well integrated with one another.

Thanks to PI®, the organization has come to realize the importance of defining both job profiles and the characteristics of the individuals who might fill them to ensure that each member is interacting in the best possible way. Today, Big Brothers Big Sisters of Canada® asks every potential employee to complete the PI® on his second round of interviews. They then compare each candidate's results with those of the PI®'s companion job-assessment tool the Performance Requirements Options®.

The organization is also turning to PI® to better exploit its complement of offsite employees by using it to tap into motivation and direction. At Big Brothers Big Sisters of Canada®, this approach has proven very capable of addressing employment gaps and identifying individuals' areas of interest.

THE SCIENCE OF HUMAN RESOURCES

The academic study of personality and the application of personality theory to the business of key organizational challenges have much to teach the professional workforce, particularly in times of evolving patterns of work, and widespread economic hardship. With so much at stake right now, businesses are looking beyond traditional HR management practices and exploring more scientific, data-driven technological solutions to managing their people. Even the Canadian government's Service Canada has seen the advantages of using behavioral assessments, declaring on its website, "Through proper use, pre-hire assessments will greatly increase hiring effectiveness as they improve the firm's ability to make precise, objective and accurate hiring decisions about an applicant's compatibility with the competencies required for a specific position."

UNITED STATES GOVERNMENT (EEOC) "RULES OF THE ROAD" FOR USING TESTING

The U.S. Equal Employment Opportunity Commission (EEOC) is responsible for enforcing federal laws that make it illegal to discriminate against a job applicant or an employee because of the person's race, color, religion, sex (including pregnancy), national origin, age, disability, or genetic information. It is also illegal to discriminate against someone because she complained about discrimination, filed a charge of discrimination, or participated in an employment discrimination investigation or lawsuit. Tests and other selection procedures can be a very effective means of determining which applicants or employees are most qualified for a particular job. However, using these tools can violate federal anti-discrimination laws if an employer intentionally does so to discriminate based on any of the above-noted qualifiers.

Ultimately, there are two elements in play when it comes to assessing the appropriateness of an individual for a position: behavior assessment (which measures a person's essential personality) and skills assessment (which measures her body of knowledge, skillset, and powers of judgment). Coincidentally (or perhaps not so much), these two markers correspond smartly with the nature-versus-nurture debate. Behavioral assessments take stock of people's innate disposition, while skills assessment takes it for a real-life run. The net result is a comprehensive snapshot that offers up valuable scientific data that managers might apply in the hiring, coaching, training, and general oversight of their human resources.

In a Cornell University HR Review, January 2013 report, (see http://www.cornellhrreview.org/personality-tests-in-employment-selection-use-with-caution) we see that when companies make poor hiring decisions, this has incredible costs to the enterprise. A bad hire not only has the potential to create a toxic workplace environment, but it can be expensive. Every bad hiring decision can cost a business 1.5 times to 5 times that employee's salary and benefits. This assumes a typical line level employee with a $50,000 combined salary and benefits, the bad hire will cost an employer at least an additional $75,000 to $80,000. From our experience, even though an employer may be challenged in court for using personality tests in employee selection, the benefits of more successful employees by far will outweigh potential legal costs. The key is for employers to use valid, reliable, and legally sustainable tests in hiring employees. We have seen time and time again that this will reduce potential lawsuits, add to diversity, and is the only way that employers can scientifically identify the best candidates for the job.

BEHAVIORAL ASSESSMENTS

The most practical branch of behavioral science, behavioral assessments explore the peculiarities of individuals' behavior. The empirical data they throw into the mix bring the full weight of scientific study to bear on the very human landscape so many bosses might be surprised to discover themselves negotiating.

In recent years, the use of validated human assessments tools has experienced a serious surge. The medically-minded and non-psychologists alike lend their voices to support the idea that individuals' personal qualities and characteristics have a crucial impact on their performance at work. This reality is reflected in an examination of job postings that indicate employers' pursuit of personality-driven factors in their would-be staffers, including social skills, initiative, creativity, and flexibility. And they seek these qualities at least as often, if not more so, as they seek specific technical skills, experience, and intellectual abilities.

That personality really matters in talent attraction and retention has become an increasingly popular view. Science has made contact with human capital—and it's about time. The better companies, of course, have known about its value for many years. Our oldest client, a privately held leader in manufacturing, packaging, shipping, and retailing based in eastern Canada, has turned to the Predictive Index® for every people-based decision for the past 40 years. All managers are trained in using identified employee behavior and drive to influence company effectiveness and increase shareholder value.

Behavioral assessments are accurate predictors of human behavior. They give insight into how a person will behave over the long haul, and so have much to offer supervisors in charge of a body of personalities, each with its own unique dimensions and descriptors. Data eliminate guesswork and provide concrete "intel" on an individual's unique dynamics.

Managers of professional organizations, no matter how disparate their particular preoccupations might seem, actually grapple with exactly the same challenges in their quotidian lives. Indeed, they likely ask themselves the same questions (or should) on a pretty regular basis. Among them, find:

- Who do I hire? I need a person quickly and they must fit our culture.

- Who do I promote? I need a successor in many roles.

- Who is my next leader? And as for the ones we don't select, how do we keep them?

- How do I keep my people engaged? With a disengagement rate of 52 percent (says a Gallup 2011 study), we need a plan.

- How do I motivate my people? With tenure comes complacency. We need to break this.

- How do I bring my team together? Teams that are jazzed do more.

- How are my people going to react to change? Safe is too risky today.

- How do I impact performance every day? Influencing must be unique to the person. All personalities are different and need to be treated uniquely.

- How does my management style impact my people? Am I a wolf or a lamb?

Conventionally speaking, business leaders have tackled these questions with the twin tools of common sense and trial-and-error. The results have been dubious, at best.

Behavior assessment offers an alternative whose foundation is reassuringly cemented in science. Here, the mounting complexities of the modern workplace are acknowledged with data that precisely matches job functions with individual characteristics, always with an eye to creating a more perfectly populated professional environment.

PUTTING BEHAVIOR ANALYSIS ON ICE

Tim Whitehead, a former NCAA Division I hockey coach, is a great example of how leaders can use behavior analyses at work. Coach Whitehead, now retired from NCAA hockey, is teaching at Kimball Union Academy, a prep school in New Hampshire, and was with the University of Maine's NCAA men's varsity hockey program for 12 winning seasons. Famous for his ability to find, train, and coach top hockey talent from around the globe, he put together a continued winning program, and his coaches and players regularly compete at the very best level in North American college hockey. The coach vies with over 50 other programs to attract the top players to his university with the knowledge that, with the right talent, coaching and winning get a whole lot easier. The need to use "employee big data" like the Predictive Index® is seen by this leader as an absolute advantage.

As an NCAA coach, Whitehead knew he needed to have the intimate understanding of his players with which the PI® has afforded him since he first tapped into its competencies in 2008. Appreciative of the college-sports truism that says the only impediment to the fast-paced action upon which successful hockey is built is a lack of communication, he's applied it to getting his players to work better as a team. Additionally, Whitehead has used its teachings to get more from his players according to anticipated responses to specific situations. And his new understanding of how "each individual student is wired" has seen the coach use hockey as leverage to keep his players focused on school so they might maintain the minimum grade level required to keep them on the team. Finally, Whitehead used the PI® to facilitate better communication among the differently skilled members of the team's management staff.

"PI® really confirms your instincts as a coach," Whitehead says. "It's fascinating knowing how our 30 players are broken up into different personalities and how I might connect better with a group of them, while the assistant coach will connect with yet another group." Thanks to this tool, Whitehead has an enhanced understanding of "which players I can get in their face, and which others to take aside."

Coach Whitehead calls the use of behavioral analytics, the Predictive Index®, and PI® a "slam-dunk" decision. The ability to have a seventh player (namely, the PI® data) to assist in insights into his players and coaching staff is essential. Whitehead uses the Predictive Index® reports to create a communication plan for his team. By spending some time getting to know how to deliver messages with impact and influence to his assistant coaches and players, he has accelerated his success. There has been no downside. The team's winning record is the measure of achievement and, having watched him in several coaching events, it's clear to me that this coach's players would go through a wall for him. He has created an ecosystem that any corporate business would love to have.

SELLING APPLE PIE TO AMERICANS

When the changing global economy and skyrocketing prices of baking supplies started to make principals at Chudleigh's Ltd., a hugely successful apple farm and bakery in Milton, Ontario, nervous a few years back, they committed to finding strategies for growth and product differentiation. It was vital, they told their employees, that they gain a better understanding of their customers and global purchasing behaviors if they hoped to continue.

Enter the Predictive Index®. The company of 100 full-timers — the numbers swell to 300 during the August-to-December peak season — today employs the PI® to measure such characteristics as dominance, extroversion, patience, and formality in its staffers so they'll understand Chudleigh's culture and know how to be successful in the marketplaces they're entering.

Thanks to the PI®, the customer benefits from the mutual interaction of salespeople more than ever. Rather than delivering a rigid pitch, Chudleigh's sellers now understand the need to solve customers' problems, quickly assessing the situation and adapting their proposal accordingly. What's more, the sales folks have upped their roles to innovator status, and have themselves developed clever new products with a novel twist. The Chudleigh pineapple upside-down cakes and lava cakes are both the brainchildren of Chudleigh's sales force.

In spite of the slow economy, the 2010 fall season was one of Chudleigh's most productive and efficient ever. It surpassed its targets in peak season consistently by 7,000 cases and added a further 25,000 square feet to its production facility. And the company consistently uses the PRO® and PI® to maintain a turnover rate that's lower than 2 percent. "There are a lot of factors working against us, with the [global] economy being the big factor," Brent Winterton, vice-president of quality assurance and human resources, has said. "So we have to be incredibly competitive and strategic and PI® helps us. Predictive Index® is a time-saver that creates an expedient way to get to the right person as soon as you can."

MOTIVATION AND HUMAN BEHAVIOR

Behavior scientists have conducted vast tracts of research into the subject of motivation and human behavior. The result is a set of behavioral models against which particular situations might be measured. While much of that research is densely technical, there are some general observations on which most scientists working in the field agree:

- Our behavior is governed by two types of interactions: those that come naturally (instincts) and those that are learned (conditioning).

- Conditioning begins early in our lives and drives major changes in subsequent behavior based upon the variety and quality of our experiences.

- All things being equal, a particular individual will behave in the same way today as he did yesterday (and will behave the same way tomorrow).

- No individual does anything until and unless he is first motivated to do so. Which triggers stir those motivational juices is a variable that's unique to each of us (and our own perceived needs). One person's perceptions of need cannot motivate another.

The net takeaway from these universal truths in which managers should find particular value is that each and every one of the souls operating under their jurisdiction is driven by different incentives, enthusiasms, and stimuli. To imagine otherwise is first day stuff in Management 101.

Still, it's right to assume that human beings do share certain universal sources of motivation that traverse the party lines. To wit, behavioral science has identified the following common themes that egg on the lot of us:

- *Goals.* Humans are goal-oriented creatures, so the targets they set for themselves tend to spur them on.

- *Pursuit of pleasure/avoidance of pain.* Humans will naturally seek out positive outcomes and steer clear of negative ones.

- *Mastery and control.* Humans prefer mastery and control to ambiguity and uncertainty. Their states of mind on these measures impact their confidence and efficiency.

- *Variety and interest.* Humans gravitate toward occupations that are stimulating and satisfying, and give a wide berth to things that are boring, stressful, or repetitive.

- *Social context.* Humans are social creatures by nature, and so a condition of social interaction and comparison is a constant. In this realm, humans are motivated both to get ahead *and* to get along.

Each of us is motivated by each of these factors to a differing degree. One person may be highly motivated by the chance to gain mastery over something while another might prefer the easier life that comes with letting someone else call the shots. And so on. Pay attention.

ASKING QUESTIONS: BEHAVIORAL SURVEYS

A key concept in behavioral assessment is the behavioral survey. Essentially an inventory of the psychological characteristics of an individual or group of individuals, these provide a measurable means of comparing the performance of different personality types at different jobs. Behavioral surveys take as fact that human behavior is both predictable and consistent. Their value as a personnel-management tool, however, is predicated largely on the time investment they require. Adults get bored with longer surveys. Our research has shown that if a survey takes over 15 minutes, the person doing it will start to act in a nonconforming or dishonest manner. The shorter the survey, we've determined, the higher the levels of completion. The Predictive Index® takes fewer than 12 minutes, providing significant objective data to make employee selection much easier and the success dramatically more predictable. It has global acceptance in better-managed companies in both for-profit and nonprofit environments.

Given that a managerial changeup is almost as inevitable as death and taxes for an evolving startup, behavioral surveys are important for the insight they offer into why some people demonstrate the capacity for entrepreneurial and innovative behavior, while others don't. That's useful material, particularly given the all-too-prevalent examples of organizations promoting individuals to posts for which they're utterly unsuitable. Behavioral surveys allow management to better understand the natural talents and motivating forces of each employee — and to lay down a unique career path that best capitalizes on them.

BUSINESS APPLICATIONS OF BEHAVIORAL SCIENCE

Forward-thinking companies understand the value of these tools and seek to both quantify and qualify workers' individual characteristics. Leaders of these firms employ behavioral science in the following ways:

- *To make hiring decisions.* The hallmark of a successful hire is a powerful fit between an employee's natural abilities and the requirements of a particular post. Other key components of the selection process include performance criteria and specific experience, training, and skills. Data gleaned from behavioral assessments can also be put to work crafting ads to attract candidates to a particular opening, and even to develop key interview questions for the next stage. When companies have set up what I call a "true north" benchmark of the key behaviors and drives needed in a role, and validated them against the current mission and sound-checked them with a data tool like Predictive Index®, predictable success in hiring A players is substantially elevated.

- *To motivate employees.* It's a given, and a constant, that employers need to light the particular fire under each of their staffers that'll get them sparked for what's required of the position. Such attention produces a higher-performing workplace and a more contented worker. A profound understanding of what motivates employees allows managers to act as interveners, muscling into the scene as needed with spot-on training, coaching, and mentoring. When you get into the world of your employees and coach from their behavioral drives, you become a better coach.

- *To provide job feedback.* It's long been understood that workers respond to managers' feedback with increased productivity and higher levels of on-the-job satisfaction. Knowing that his work has been acknowledged and appreciated boosts a staffer's sense of self-esteem and security. Alternatively, insufficient communication with subordinates creates a climate of fear and mistrust. Morale plummets and a culture of negativity takes root in the place. This is particularly so in times of upheaval or change. Ultimately, it's incumbent on a manager to bridge the divide between his own comfort level with such communication, and his workers' need for the same.

- *To manage conflict.* Throw a group of disparate personalities into the same space and stand by for disagreement. Behavioral assessment can provide vital objective information about what festers at its root. More than that, it offers a clinically-removed means of discussing difficult situations so that no one is threatened by the conversation. By bridging the conflict with data, both parties feel respected and heard, and thus are heartened by the prospect of resolving outstanding issues. Managers, meanwhile, can focus on the human analytics behind the discord rather than the issue itself. This kind of scientific approach also sets the organization up for tackling conflict in the longer term.

- *To team-build.* Effective teams—whether they exist in sports organizations or C-suites—share certain characteristics. They all value communication and have honed their proficiency with it. They understand that the better teams don't all look alike, that they include players who challenge the communication process and sidestep "group think." Everyone has a handle on decision-making, and they're all as productive as they are positive. The key to unlocking such an idyll is an appreciation for how people work together. Behavioral assessment helps to provide objective information about the motivational characteristics and work behaviors of individual group members. Their revelations help a manager to account for the gaps and maximize the strengths of each of his team members.

- *To manage performance.* Performance-management is often about helping an employee to do more or less of a particular aspect of his role with a view to improving overall performance. With behavioral assessment, managers understand the motivators behind current behaviors and, thus equipped with real data, can look to impact change from an authentic base. Whether delivering tough feedback to an account manager or inspiring a sales rep to push harder, managers can use the information contained in behavioral assessments to approach the issue in a style that will be best received by their audience.

- *To coach.* One-on-one coaching is an important way that executive team members develop the skills that will cultivate stronger relationships among them. The data revealed by behavioral assessments throws wide a person's natural conduct and workplace preferences. Layer this with what a manager has uncovered about his own behavioral requirements and communication style and produce a perfect storm of contextual data points and laser-focused coaching.

- *To effect structural changes.* Mergers, acquisitions, and restructurings are all chapters inside a typical company's story. Thanks to the powers of behavioral assessments, data-based decision-making becomes a new reality. With it, organizations understand the natural ways, styles, and relational tactics of both current and potential leaders. At Predictive Success, we've used behavior data from the Predictive Index® to help many companies expedite the merger process. Most mergers fail. But introducing a Predictive Index® people plan provides a robust, data-driven path for putting the right people in the right roles in the new organization quickly in what employees tell us is a fair, objective process.

- *To retain employees.* Along with talent acquisition, talent retention endures as a priority throughout the life cycle of each employee. By understanding the peculiarities of their existing workforce, managers take significant steps to keep them engaged and happy on the ship. And the payout for such diligence is big and indisputable: reduced costs associated with high turnover, lost opportunity, productivity, and morale. Employees leave their supervisors, so those supervisors looking to retain their workforce must get equipped with a process that spurs its members' drives and motivations.

- *To plan for succession.* A critical component of every organization's long view, succession planning can benefit meaningfully from the gifts behavioral assessments have to offer. In combination with experience, interests, and education, the data revealed in a behavior assessment can identify those individuals primed for future promotion.

BEHAVIORAL ASSESSMENTS IN REVERSE

There is application for the Predictive Index® at the other end of the scale, too. With the increased understanding of an individual's personal skills, strengths, and preferences that this special tool reveals, identifying the best pick for your next career move is a breeze. The case of a woman named Kelly Golby provides an excellent example of this in action.

Golby had 14 years of retail fashion experience and her own about-to-close boutique when she stumbled across the powers of this job-assessment tool. The career search that followed her decision to shut down her store was an exercise in frustration, even in spite of Golby's impressive skillset, retail fashion experience, and demonstrated ability to manage large teams. Then she took the Predictive Index® and the results opened her eyes.

Before PI®, although she knew that she liked sales and had significant experience in management and administration, Golby lacked the confidence to expand into other areas. But her PI® results confirmed that she should. They helped her direct her energy and focus her job search to arenas in which she had the greatest chance of success. So it was that Golby landed a plum post as a sales associate at Michael Kors in Holt Renfrew, fortified for the encounter by the "constructive positive language" of her PI® report. Indeed, when she handed the Michael Kors representative her PI® results at the job interview, it sealed the deal. Holt Renfrew also employs this behavior analysis technique, and they were pleased to discover their findings matched hers.

AN ASSESSMENT OF BEHAVIORAL ASSESSMENTS

American research and market intelligence firm Aberdeen Group (Boston, Massachusetts) recently polled more than 640 organizations — including 516 who currently use behavioral assessments as part of their talent strategy — to try to understand the effectiveness of this tool. The results demonstrate that such a systematic approach is measurably useful in enhancing the performance of employees.

In examining those companies it considers "best in class," Aberdeen discovered a powerful common thread. Each of them put their faith in the sanctity of the data with which the assessments furnished them. Across the board, at every decision-making opportunity, these organizations turned to that data and let the data assist them in achieving consensus.

Researchers also identified several other characteristics that these winning companies share. Prominent among them were:

- Their use of assessments as a tool to drive better talent decisions at multiple points in the employee life cycle.

- Collaboration between HR and the business to create a language of competencies inside which assessment can occur.

- Their employment of a variety of assessment types, appropriate to the decision at hand, to help minimize the risk in critical talent determinations.

- Their use of assessment data to help identify talent gaps and available talent resources to support long-term workforce and business planning.

- Their practice of assessing not only for current skills, but also for future leadership and development potential.

The Aberdeen research concluded that, "as every business decision falls under greater scrutiny, organizations are looking for tools that help them make better choices." Assessments can provide valuable insights into hiring, promotion, and development decisions, and help organizations minimize talent risk while maximizing talent performance.

PICKING A BEHAVIORAL ASSESSMENT APPROACH

Candidate, functional, neonatal, PDA, even canine: All are subsets inside the larger category of behavioral assessments — and the glut of options is further bulked up by the vast numbers of vendors marketing the tools. In some cases, respondents are forced to select whatever answers most "closely" represent them, in the absence of an exact match. Many of the vendors lack any science behind their tool. Many are copycat, nonvalidated knockoffs of someone else's research, plagiarized and tweaked just enough to avoid litigation. These invite risk to the companies that use them and a quick buck for the unscrupulous vendors who hawk them.

Then there's the old standby, Myers Briggs (which is not validated for selection), wherein employees and managers are assigned a quartet of letters that tell a story about their personality. But some consider such a system unwieldy, and complain that manager and employee — both — have forgotten their pigeonholes by the time such information might become useful.

In my experience, the best tools tend to come from the "free-choice" assessment academic camp, like the Predictive Index®. Its quick turnaround applicability and simple, two-question, adjective-listing style work well for business. That the test allows its administrators to gain objective data that's not threatening to either implement or use is essential. And, again, it's wise to bear in mind the attention spans of your test-taking demographic, and to recognize the limited interest lots of folks will have in sitting down to complete 45- to 90-minute personality assessments that research has shown they consider intrusive.

Given the amount of choice on the market for testing it's important to remember that all behavioral assessments are not created equal. To be appropriate for business use, they should possess the following quartet of characteristics: reliability (the measuring instrument needs to be consistent and stable such that it yields the same results each time it measures the same personality trait); validity (a measurement instrument is valid if it measures what it purports to measure, and can prove it with empirical data); an absence of adverse impacts (in other words, the instrument is free from bias and doesn't put any one population slice at a disadvantage over another); and compliance (because we're wandering in the world of business, and compliance with those government regulations that oversee hiring and HR matters is essential).

THE PRODUCTIVITY AMBITION MATRIX

The productivity ambition matrix is a construct that considers the evolving requirements of managers as they shift from being individual contributors (ICs) to leaders of others. As their roles expand, so too does their need for new awareness and skills. They must, essentially, move upstream in their ambitions to be more productive. Where the IC was okay with her own core personality as revealed by a deep dive into her own Predictive Index®, a leader's transition to managing others calls for an ambition to be a learner.

Ultimately, success awaits the leader who is self-aware. The person who rock-solid knows his own drives and motivations simply has an advantage in interpersonal communications over the guy who exists in a cloud of self-deception. The first step here is adopting a policy of open and honest dialogue with oneself to produce a state of core optimization in the productivity ambition matrix. After this is achieved, he can move to his adjacent critical connections with a better game plan for success. Visually, this expansive process looks like increasing half moons resonating out from one's core personality to those he needs to influence.

It's important to be self-aware regarding one's levels of dominance, extroversion, patience, detail, and empathy in this exercise. Communication can be difficult at the best of times, and when people are under stress, they gravitate to their own style. If they're naturally assertive, they become more aggressive. If they're extroverted, they become more persuasive and given to "selling." And if they're naturally sequential and detail-oriented in nature, they retreat to their data-hungry and risk-averse orientation.

Bullying won't work to get you into the world of the folks you're trying to sway; what works better is a data-driven approach that acknowledges a call for ambition. The use of behavior data like those upturned in the Predictive Index® only enhances both the delivery and the reception of messages and delivers us to the productive realm of "third-box thinking." It is here that we might study the behavior patterns of those we speak to after examining their Predictive Index® report and compare their preferred communication path to ours. From my experience with the more than 3,000 leaders I've trained in predictive modeling, this process has increased the acceptance rates of influencing action dramatically.

With Predictive Index® data, an individual can advance to the transformational communication circle — and there lies the top of the productivity matrix. This rich media space of critical connections is where all the decisions get set out and actually implemented (or not). Here — the

highest region in the matrix; the big ROI of transformational communication—the leader who is able to
calibrate his universe, drive, and motivations, *in addition
to* those of his employees, arrives in triumph. This is the
place where people will go through the wall for each
other, where productivity and fun are mainstays of work,
and where drama disappears. It's not easy getting here,
but it sure is worth the trip.

9

How to Engage

ACADEMICS AND BUSINESS FOLK ALIKE HAVE LONG argued for
the merits of an engaged workforce. The company that has
one, they say, has a competitive advantage over the company that doesn't. And indeed, a mass of data makes the
case for organizations with a handle on employee engagement outperforming their less absorbed competition.
With engaged employees, it seems, great companies find
meaningful distinction from merely good ones. As such,
successful engagement of employees has emerged among
the most critical imperatives of an effective leader.

THE ENGAGEMENT ANXIETY

Google "what employers worry about" and prepare to be
stunned by the utter plainness of the results. Far from a
litany of extravagant and convoluted management con-
cepts whose absence from their organizations one might

imagine business leaders to be lamenting, the identified concerns are actually focused on the very lifeblood of managers' professional existence: their employees.

In "Retention of Key Talent and the Role of Rewards," a survey of 526 HR professionals recently undertaken by WorldatWork, a not-for-profit organization providing education and research focused on global HR issues, the majority of senior-management respondents — 74 percent — cited identification of key talent as the most effective tactic for retaining staffers.

Among the reasons the survey found for employees leaving their jobs, lack of opportunity for training and development figured large — in other words, workers feeling disengaged by an ongoing diet of more of the same. Manpower Group's Right Management, meanwhile, also singled out low engagement among the most pressing challenges companies currently face. For almost one in every five of the survey's respondents, losing strong performers who feel less than charmed with their present employer is the biggest anxiety. "This is the kind of concern," Right's senior vice-president of talent management, Michael Haid, has said, "that HR people lose sleep over."

DEFINING THE ENGAGED EMPLOYEE

An engaged employee is a person who's fully involved in, and entirely enthusiastic about, her job. Our research has shown that when an employee is engaged, she has fewer days away from work, is productive, and suffers fewer accidents. This person approaches her work with passion and feels a profound emotional connection to her employer. But bear in mind: sometimes, people are *happy* at work, but aren't *engaged* with it. Sometimes employee satisfaction surveys reveal workers to be relatively content with their daily tasks, but not emotionally tied into the results they seek to achieve. That's a problem.

In his book, *Getting Engaged: The New Workplace Loyalty*, author Tim Rutledge explains that people who are genuinely engaged with their work are attracted to and inspired by it (as in, "I *want* to do this"), fascinated by it (as in, "I *love* what I'm doing"), and committed to it (as in, "I'm dedicated to the success of what I'm doing").

Another mark of an engaged employee is the level of exertion she's prepared to put into her job. When employees are *engaged* with the work they do, they employ *discretionary effort* in its execution. That means they dig deep into their own bag and apply whatever's called for to get the task at hand done—even in the absence of any apparent promise of immediate reward. These are the conscientious workers who perform at a higher level than they might, regardless of whether the eyes of company brass are upon them, putting in overtime, delivering beyond the call, looking after responsibilities that aren't necessarily within their purview. These are the players you want on your team.

WHY IS ENGAGEMENT IMPORTANT?

An old joke that makes the rounds at business breakfasts and golf outings has lots to say about the value of cultivating an engaged workforce—and about the startling deficit that currently exists on this count. In the quip, a CEO is asked how many people work in his company. "About half of them," goes the response. The moral of the joke is simple: if employees aren't engaged in their work, they're wasting time, money, resources, and potential.

Not surprisingly, the value of employee engagement is ultimately tracked back to the bottom line. A whack of case studies reveals the dollar value of an engaged workforce to the company at its helm. According to one bit of research, one category of "actively disengaged" account executives at the American specialty mortgage banking company New Century Financial Corporation produced 28 percent less revenue than their engaged associates.

"To win in the marketplace," former Campbell's Soup CEO Doug Conant once said, "you must first win in the workplace." Indeed. And so get your staffers hooked on your organization, and they'll deliver victory to your efforts. Among the many ancillary wins, consider:

- Engaged employees arrive on the job with an appetite for the requirements that lie ahead of them. These people actually *like* what they do—a detail whose worth can't be underestimated in an overarching assessment of a labor force's performance.

- Engaged employees have been shown to possess a strong sense of purpose for the work they do. This measure has also been demonstrated to have an effect on staffers' mindsets. Engaged employees fiercely believe that their part in a company-wide initiative can make a genuine difference in the organization that employs them. This transports us to the important realm of spirituality on the job, and the value a solid dose of the stuff has on company productivity.

- Engaged employees have a genuine interest in pleasing your clients. They'll go the distance to enhance the customer experience, they'll provide better service, and they'll produce higher-quality products. Happy customers will hang around longer and spend more. At the end of this domino trail, you'll find higher levels of profit and richer shareholder returns.

- Engaged employees have longer tenure tracks. That means the demands of restaffing and the costs of turnover are minimized.

- Engaged employees are worth more. One study by Hay Group found that companies with highly engaged workers grew revenues at a rate two-and-a-half times higher than those with low engagement levels. Another, this by Towers Perrin, found companies with engaged workers had 6 percent higher net profit margins. And HR consultancy Kenexa discovered that organizations with engaged workforces enjoyed shareholder returns, over a five-year period that were five times higher than their less connected counterparts. Research we have done at Predictive Success shows that employees who are engaged have fewer accidents at work and are absent from work far less.

EMPLOYEE ENGAGEMENT: A HOW-TO

Leaders of workforces whose members demonstrate high levels of engagement behave differently from their counterparts when it comes to managing their people. Full stop. Here are eight tips on how to be more like them:

1. *Solicit feedback from your staff.* The number of workers who would not recommend their place of employment to a friend is alarming. A recent survey of the subject in the United States by the *Gallup Management Journal* discovered that just 29 percent of employees are actively engaged in their jobs, and 54 percent are not engaged. That's crisis territory. Only by inquiring can a manager comprehend the reputation his organization has with its people. Ask

the questions. Undertake 360 surveys like the LPI, Leadership Performance Index. See http://predictive success.com/solutions/multiple-source-development-survey/. In our experience, input from your boss and the people you lead includes both negative and positive blind spots. If your negative blind spots are greater than your positive ones, your development roadmap reveals itself. An example of a multi-development survey (like a 360-degree report) is shown in Figures 9.1 and 9.2.

2. *Provide feedback to your staff.* Effective leaders establish processes and procedures that help people master important tasks. And they enhance these efforts with regular performance reports. Remember, though: when a leader delivers feedback to an employee with the employee's behaviors at its core, that feedback will be listened to more robustly than it otherwise might, because it's delivered from *their* worldview, not yours.

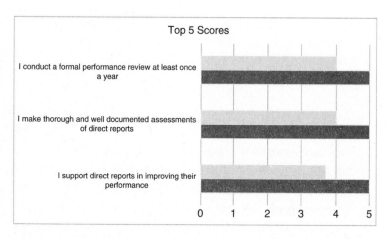

Figure 9.1   Example of a 360 Survey LPI, Leadership Performance Index

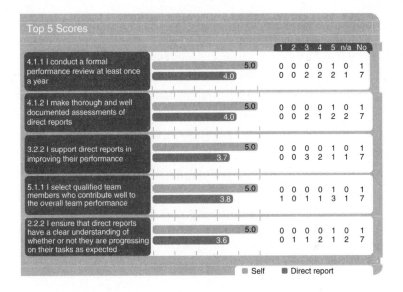

Figure 9.2   Leadership Performance Index, LPI

3. *Solicit feedback from your internal and external customers.* That means acknowledging their compliments, yes, but also addressing their complaints. A management strategy that stays alive to positives and negatives, and builds both responses into an ever-evolving set of employment practices, stays relevant.

4. *Always be clear.* Embracing this ABC is essential to success. Senior leadership that is explicit with its expectations will fare much better than those that offer only muddy instructions. If you haven't been properly prepared for reaching an objective, after all, you'll feel unmotivated to do so.

5. *Provide rich opportunities.* Employees who work for managers who've made a commitment to job advancement and new prospects will reward them in kind. Most people want to be challenged on the job.

Managers ignore this reality to their own potential detriment. In other words, don't put a personality who needs variety with a personality who needs independence into a cubical together to crunch out reports eight hours a day and expect an engaged, productive employee.

6. *Institute smart performance measures* that enhance — not damage — the work you've done. Call centers that assess staffers according to their call count risk inviting trouble by not allowing call takers the time they need to adequately address complex issues. Rather than judging performance according to time or cost, identify those factors that will increase customer loyalty, say. Call centers that reward employees according to the calls they resolve successfully inside a single encounter have a smarter focus. Mapping people to roles allows for higher performance.

7. *Encourage collaboration.* Studies show that employees who work in teams outperform individuals. Great leaders are team builders, and the environment they establish cultivates trust and partnerships. At airline firm JetBlue, management pushes a system of "desired behaviors" designed to boost customer service via group effort. Pilots, flight attendants, and gate agents are equally required to join forces to clean the main cabin, for example. That way, the twin imperatives of cabin cleanliness and quick between-flight turnaround are achieved by every party with an interest in them. Everyone is accountable; no one holds the bag.

8. *Connect with your workforce.* Free Friday lunches and on-site gyms are one thing, but employees who suffer troubled relationships with their superiors simply won't put out at the same level as employees who

feel a bond. Relate to your employees on their level. Obtaining data on engagement is essential to keeping employees happy and jazzed at work. Your better employees have choices out there and, in the decade to come, more options to leave the supervisor who treats them poorly. Your bottom-performing workers stay in role, and these C players become energy vampires with very little upside in their development potential or productivity lift for the business.

THE ROLE BEHAVIOR ANALYSES HAVE TO PLAY

Research on employee engagement suggests that its success is very much a function of the breadth and depth of information that managers have been able to gather on their subordinates. The more business leaders understand about the personalities that work beneath them, the more likely they'll be able to engage them. And so it is that the requirement for leaders to identify the level of engagement in their organization—and then to implement behavioral strategies that will facilitate *full* engagement—is more important than ever.

Employee workplace satisfaction is an essential element of custom personality assessments and the powers they deliver to a business environment. The truths they uncover have much to say about how probable it is that an employee will feel fulfilled by his professional obligations—and will be more productive as a result.

This is why it's important for managers to wake up and cultivate their best workers with personality and behavior assessments that better match their skills, character types, and professional preferences to the tasks at hand.

The most successful business leaders, after all, are the ones who are able to identify the key talent within their organizations—and to make a muscular effort to keep those employees both professionally and personally engaged on the job. Such assessments are like the extra-wide pipes that facilitate more water for growth. They increase capacity and reduce costs. By not using them, managers introduce additional risk to any business. Would you run a company without proper financials? Of course not. Then why are companies running people plans without proper objective data points on their employees?

SHARE THE WEALTH

President Woodrow Wilson was famously said to have suffered the burden of a particularly ineffective secretarial staff. It was a condition that left him multitasking like a thief, less effective than he might have been, and with his Achilles heel woefully exposed.

An inability—or unwillingness—to delegate tasks to others is an extremely critical shortcoming on the scale of managerial imperatives. Without mastering this trick, leaders open their workplaces up to frustration, time loss, confusion, motivational dearth, and a general state of corporate unproductivity. Many leaders who were great specialists in a subordinate role struggle with letting go as they move into management.

Some people are intensely uncomfortable with the idea of delegation. They either regard it as a shameful shirking of responsibility or as a dangerous loss of essential control. Both, as it turns out, are wrong. Managers who know how to delegate, a thousand different real-life examples have taught us, are actually the most opportunely situated for success. And it's not just because many hands make light work, either. It's about accurately identifying the tasks with which those hands might best occupy themselves.

Behavior analyses can detect and measure a person's ability to effectively allocate work-related tasks to others in his professional circle. There are particular traits, after all, that have been singled out as being suggestive of a delegation-friendly personality. The profile that results reveals both what people want *and* what they fear — eminently useful data for structuring an effective work environment.

At the end of the day, the extent of a person's ability to delegate is tantamount to a measure of his ability to trust. An individual who scores highly on his drive to dominate is reticent to extend *authority* to others. So debilitated by fear is this guy, he tends only to trust himself.

An individual with a high drive for formality meanwhile, is reluctant to assign *details* to others. That's largely thanks to his inherent pessimism about his own abilities, an anxiety that spills over into a broad-based distrust that anyone else could do any better.

Ideally, an organization wants to cultivate managers who are capable of allocating not only the oversight of a task's tactical execution to someone else, but the ultimate authority for its completion. The benefits from attention to this kind of thing cannot be overstated. "We all have a blind spot in some part of our eye," said Wilson's biographer Joseph Patrick Tumulty in 1921. "President Wilson's was in his inability to use men."

Clever managers should make it a goal not to be similarly sightless.

And so it is that leaders must employ behavior analyses to identify the level of engagement in their organization, to find out the reasons behind the lack of comprehensive engagement, to work — in an ongoing way — to eradicate those reasons, and to implement behavioral strategies that will facilitate across-the-board engagement within the workplace.

THE MICROSOFT EXAMPLE

Randy Lenaghan is an example of a leader who knows how to engage his employees. He famously illustrated that with a direct report statement in a year-end review in which one of his employees declared that he "would take two bullets for Randy." In his years serving as vice-president of enterprise sales at Microsoft Canada, Lenaghan won many awards for leadership skills, including many "manager of the year" honors. He was also selected to participate in the company's esteemed high-potential program. Lenaghan has always been focused on his people.

Lenaghan hates gossip and doesn't allow it. He does, however, have the opposite sentiment about objective data. He believes in objective data's powers for selecting his team, coaching his leaders, and avoiding unnecessary conflict. Lenaghan has used the PI® and its companion assessment tool, the PRO®, to take an in-depth, analytical look at his employees in pursuit of making his organization more productive and efficient. By identifying how his team was constructed from a behavioral perspective, he was able to understand how the individuals within it complemented one another, and to ultimately determine what types of behavioral styles were required to produce the most high-performing team. He found the experience enlightening. "The data showed me who was on my team and if they were in the right role," says Lenaghan. "If they were not in the right role for them, but were good for the organization, we were able to move them to a position better suited to them."

Lenaghan also used the PI® to help with his "change agenda," a rough blueprint that acknowledged that his business was evolving, and that the needs and wants of its customer base were, too. "Our idea of what made good sales professional[s] had to change, as well." With the help of the PI® and PRO®, Lenaghan has been able to build teams with more customer-centric sales professionals. In turn, revenues under Randy's leadership grew by an extraordinary $250 million in the two-year span under his watch while the organization implemented the Predictive Index® program.

EMPLOYEE ENGAGEMENT IN DOWN TIMES

In a slow-growth economy, keeping the clients you already have can mean the difference between profit and loss, sometimes survival and death. And as companies battle for loyal customers and return business, some have discovered a most effective weapon—highly engaged employees.

When employment conditions have left employees feeling anxious or overworked, that's precisely when their managers require their wholehearted commitment the most. Managing a body of disparate souls in such a way that everyone prospers can be a tough slog in the best of times, but load yourself up with the task when the economy is shaky, and you'll know real challenge.

But contrary to what your knee-jerk opinion might be, such a trying period is actually the *best* occasion to focus on your people. Now is not a time to lose focus or delay a called-for course shift just because you're reeling from the news. Nobody gets that luxury.

If your business is experiencing decreasing revenues, shrinking budgets, and increasing uncertainty, you need to wrap a silver lining around the cloud and recast it as an opportunity to reevaluate your goals, and to reacquaint your team with how their contributions will help to achieve them. Strategic talent management is more important during economic slumps than ever. By cultivating a motivated workforce whose members are occupied by those tasks for which they are most expertly suited in the lean stretches, leaders set the stage for success when the worm turns. Some tactics for seeing this rags-to-riches transformation through might include:

- Establishing (or reestablishing) clear objectives for the entire team that reflect the way that external influences are forcing your hand.

- Securing alignment within the entire workforce such that everyone is pointed in the same (newly-defined) direction.

- If you decide there's no recourse but to trim your ranks, do so mindfully, armed with as much knowledge about each individual as you can muster. Avoid the traditional across-the-board cut and look to shed dead weight only. Untargeted downsizing might deprive you of top talent and leave you with naught but mediocrity. Laying off employees is never a pleasant experience, but doing so leaves a more finely tuned, precisely applied workforce in its wake.

- Be transparent with all that you do. There's nothing that's going to disengage a worker from his labors more than a sense that his superiors are behaving in an underhanded or disingenuous fashion.

- Hire or promote to better equip your team. As counterintuitive as it might seem, downtimes are actually ideal periods for bulking up your talent pool. Having identified a new corporate direction, it's important now to optimize your resources by populating your lines with the personalities best suited to seeing it through.

- Watch your workforce for its members' behavior during your most trying times. Leaders make themselves known during turmoil. Pay attention. If you have old data, resurvey. From our experience, the use of the Predictive Index® self-concept graph (which measures employees' view of their world and their supervisors during the period the survey was taken) provides an outstanding inner view on how a company is being led in the moment. Keeping the data fresh and avoiding rearview mirror assessments just makes sense.

10

How to Resolve

CONFLICT IS A FACT OF LIFE. It happens in politics, within your family, inside the ranks of your favorite pro sports team, between the followers of religious belief systems, and, yes, in your company break room. Better leaders welcome *some* level of conflict to encourage what we call "creative destruction." The stuff actually can be effective, though managers must take care not to invite too much of it lest they invite added drama into the workplace—and this is not effective.

For some folks, the idea of conflict at work might include everything from a stink eye at the water cooler to an ongoing and long-simmering feud that decimates departments and sends morale into the septics. So much of it is a matter of perspective. Still, it's probably fair to say that if it's disrupting the flow of work in your midst, it qualifies as "conflict."

As for how much, one study revealed that a full 85 percent of employees struggle with at least some degree of conflict in the workplace, and 29 percent said they do it "always" or "frequently." While most conflict seems to brew in the more subordinate positions, with 34 percent of folks in entry-level/frontline roles counting conflict among the characteristics of their professional life, there are still plenty of clashes in the executive suites (one in eight employees report that disagreements within their senior teams are frequent or continual).

In that same study, the primary causes of workplace conflict were determined to be personality clashes and warring egos (49 percent) followed by stress (34 percent) and heavy workloads (33 percent).

THE COST OF CONFLICT

It should surprise no one that the *bad* kind of conflict, the kind that doesn't transform itself sweetly into better-for-the-skirmish resolutions, has a price tag attached to it. A British study found that the average employee spends 2.1 hours a week dealing with conflict. Multiply that bit of found truth by the number of staffers you have on the payroll and the number of working weeks in the year, and arrive at your own conclusion about the impact workplace conflict is having on your bottom line.

As for executives, it's been estimated that 42 percent of a manager's time is spent addressing conflict in the workplace. It's an extraordinary pill to swallow.

And consider the tax this kind of thing takes on a company's human resources department. The UK research uncovered a situation in which more than half of the HR workers questioned (51 percent) were spending between one and five hours a week simply managing disagreements. That's a pretty brutal statistic. Any attempts to manage in that world are bound for failure.

Bear in mind, too, that those lost employee hours—whether spent mitigating or engaging in the conflict—might not only be applied to pastimes other than arbitrating personal in-office eruptions, but to more lucrative tasks that could be drawing in cash. (Though there always exists the possibility that the conflict-resolution work could produce a better, more productive environment once the wringer has been got through.)

Conflict costs in less direct ways, too. In some cases, workplace conflict can lead to absenteeism, as foes react to the unpleasantness of the situation by flat-out staying away from it. More likely, the expense of conflict is felt in the quality of work that's produced. It stands to reason that an initiative saddled with discord is going to be less impressive than one that sails through without such hindrances.

And so it is that conflict tallies its fees to produce the ultimate price. Poorly managed conflict will send employees and customers for the hills, in equal measure. Neither is any too beneficial for the longevity of the place.

———

CONFLICT IS "GOOD"

Everybody knows a couple that claims they never fight. I know it's unusual, Mr. and Mrs. Perfect will graciously concede to their gob-smacked audience, but we simply *never* have any arguments. To them, we say, first, *Yeah, right*, and, next, *too bad*. It's from points of conflict, after all, that change takes place.

In a recent study of a segment of the British workforce, more than three-quarters of survey respondents reported that the presence of conflict in their lives—and the subsequent imperative to sort through it in some way—resulted in an outcome that actually improved the situation beyond what it was prior to the conflict. Among the possible positive fallouts from such prickly scenarios is a better understanding of others (41 percent) and a more advantageous solution to a workplace problem (81 percent).

At the heart of every conflict is a difference. It may be a difference of style, a difference of tone, a difference of preference, a difference of approach. But it is almost certainly a difference of opinion. And here's the best news: that's not a bad thing. Inject some *difference* into any situation, and know that it could consequently go either way. The difference could prove just the ticket for sending a rocky situation off the cliffs, to be sure. But it could also serve as the scene-shaking catalyst that reverses the direction of a downshift. If nothing else, conflict equals dynamism. Its unsettling presence introduces an energy that can be harnessed in a positive way.

And before you write this off as one more surprising and cheerful business aphorism that sounds likely simply on the strength of *how unlikely* it seems, think about it. Company A is an apparent picture of togetherness. The CEO is an autocrat; the workers are robots. Everybody puts their heads down here, and the work gets done. Company B has more wrinkles on its skin. Employees here feel comfortable offering their points of view, even if it means occasionally upsetting the apple cart. Sometimes, outright, full-on arguments erupt, and it takes a serious period of readjustment for order to be restored.

Which company seems more poised for progress? In which company does it seem more likely that transformative change might occur?

While never to diminish the potential for making things worse that conflict threatens a scene with, and neither to skim over those working environments that are all about an ego-obsessed leader looking for clashes at every turn, a negative outcome is not always a given. Conflict can deliver a pummeling blow to the status quo, and render a company pointedly altered in its wake. It's thanks to conflict that innovation takes place. It's thanks to conflict that novelty finds its footing. The difference between Company A and B is in its management. The leaders at the latter company welcome conflict, in the form of constructive input. They have cultivated a culture in which challenge is a happy fact of life, where constructive debate is a constant, and where differences are celebrated for the ideas they generate.

From a management point of view, conflict actually offers an organization an extremely lucrative potential for profit improvement.

THE PSYCHOLOGY OF CONFLICT

Exploiting the good kind of conflict and sidestepping the bad is ultimately a matter of understanding the psychology driving the stuff. Here's where having a solid handle on business psychology and behavior analyses can take you far. In his book *Beyond Reason*, lawyer Roger Fisher submits that corporate leaders need to dig deep into the personalities of those folks who make up their payroll, and uncover the emotional motors that are powering the disturbances. Ignoring the emotions in conflict is a recipe for, well, for enduring conflict. It is vital that every manager, and every employee working beneath him, finds a way to identify and give play to those emotions—and then to invite the kind of conversation that will air these findings generously.

Diagnostic personality-testing tools like the Predictive Index® have much to offer this process. With them, managers and HR professionals can gain valuable insight into the unique bunch of dispositions in their keeping, and employ smart approaches to encouraging them to communicate with one another.

With a system in place that acknowledges the range of types employed in the same closed quarters, and facilitates the means for their productive communion with each other, conflict enters a new dimension. Infused with unprecedented psychometric understanding, it solves underperformance issues, turns struggling teams around, and starts the most promising of conversations.

LAUGHTER'S LONG LEGACY

The maxim that our chairman at Predictive Success, John Watson, loves is *"when a person genuinely loves what she does, she's never really working."* This has always had a strong following. That perspective gets a boost with news demonstrating that the shortest route to a long life may actually be laughably easy.

According to research published recently in the journal *Aging*, a sunny outlook may be the most important predictor of human longevity. A team of scientists from the Albert Einstein College of Medicine and Ferkauf Graduate School of Psychology at Yeshiva University—both in New York City—has isolated certain personality traits as being highly predictive of long life. Various genetically-based aspects of personality, it seems, have a meaningful impact on not only health but for how long it holds out.

Honing in on 500 subjects over the age of 95, and 700 of their offspring, the researchers employed a personality scale to understand what personality markers have something to say about our lifespan. The findings—which are contrary to the popularly held notion that old folks' impressive survival rates are a function of their ornery dispositions—offer new understanding of the role people's innate temperaments have to play in a successful life. The longer-lived among us, report the scientists, consider laughter essential to their existence and are more likely to express their emotions than bottle them up.

The researchers also found that the study participants scored lower on tests for neurotic personality and higher on those measuring conscientiousness, compared with the scores of the balance of the population.

The news is further confirmation of the importance of accounting for individuals' unique personalities — through smart behavior-analysis tools — in identifying the most productive paths for their lives. By collecting such data on corporate staffers, managers create a baseline of objectivity from which conflict can be tackled. At Predictive Success we call this "Critical Connection Mapping." Our Managing Principals create this for the clients to create sightlines to better communication routing.

THINK ABOUT IT

It's surprising to review the arc of behavioral psychology's evolution in the world, and acknowledge how little of it has consumed itself with the business of our working lives. Considering that the majority of our waking hours are spent at the office (or at the warehouse, factory floor, or whatever setting makes up one's employed backdrop), it's a given that we bring our own singular collection of idiosyncrasies and preferences, talents and shortcomings, attitudes and behavioral ticks to bear on the work at hand. What madness to ignore these things, especially considering the stew of them that mix toxically together inside a manager's oversight.

To make sure their workforces are operating at optimal levels and to promote growth, some companies have taken to hiring individuals trained in industrial and organizational psychology. This area of behavioral science is devoted to the study of human beings' relationships with their jobs and how the intimate and personal details of their working tendencies inform their organization as a whole. Industrial and organizational psychologists are interested in subjects like recruitment, the enhancement of employee skills, the institution of fair workplace procedures, employee motivation, and employee well-being.

Well-equipped with a scholarly understanding of employee behaviors and attitudes, these guys take a scientific approach to studying the psychological phenomena that are at play in the professional environment, and to applying this knowledge to improve productivity and the quality of life on the job. They advise companies on how this might take place through enhanced hiring practices, designated training programs, and more thoughtfully devised and delivered employee feedback.

Self-assessment tools are also extremely valuable for understanding why particular personalities clash, and for helping administrators to delicately extricate the parties from the conflict.

THE PREDICTIVE INDEX®, EXPLAINED

The Predictive Index®, (PI®)) assessment tool is a stellar example of this kind of thing. This scientifically-validated management instrument offers a fresh understanding of individuals' needs and drives with a view to helping business leaders to identify, retain, and develop their key talent for long-term results. The PI® is founded in science and developed for everyday use, and is versatile enough to be used across all levels of an organization, from hiring an hourly employee to selecting future leaders.

Developed in 1955, the Predictive Index® (PI®) looks to predict workplace behavior according to the results of a brief adjective checklist undertaken by each employee. Their responses provide managers with detailed information about what makes people tick by overlaying them across an extensive library of 500-plus criterion-related job validity studies covering numerous jobs and industries. The Predictive Index® (PI®) thus offers a clear understanding of the unique behavioral needs and drives that motivate their employees.

More than just a selection tool, the Predictive Index®, provides managers with ongoing insight into the psyches of their subordinates throughout the employee lifecycle, such that they might employ it to drive performance through improved communication and employee development, among other things.

A recent article in the Canadian national newspaper, *the Globe and Mail*, penned by a journalist whose own test results found him to be "cautious," "conservative," "detail-oriented," and possessed of a "logic-based" decision style, celebrated the competencies of the Predictive Index®.

"If I was applying for a job at a company that subscribed to Predictive Index®, this would be crucial information to see if I match the traits my potential employer has decided are crucial in the position. A bad fit and I'd be back pounding the pavement," the author Richard Blackwell writes.

The piece goes on to point out that psychological testing has emerged as a powerful tool for companies as a quick way to figure out who's best suited for which position. "Those who use it say it has improved their recruitment dramatically, and sharply reduces costly errors in hiring employees who just don't fit with their corporate culture."

In an example cited in the piece, Ron Hyson, vice-president of HR at Markham, Ontario-based Sofina Foods, an emerging North American leader in food service (where Predictive Index® is the brand standard for all hiring activities), extols its virtues. "It doesn't eliminate mistakes," Hyson's quoted as saying, "but we make much better hiring decisions." He likes that the test ensures that staffers don't get taken on in positions they don't really relish doing. "If a person is outgoing and likes dealing with people, but is applying for a job that mainly involves internal paperwork, the test will raise red flags."

THE ISAT™/SSAT™, REVEALED

But once you have the right behaviors, how do you train them?

Like the PI, ISAT or Influencing Skills Assessment Tool and the SSAT, Sales Skilss Assessment Tool measure abilities. Both provide powerful insights on how a leader or salesperson's behavior impacts performance. These sophisticated instruments will actually produce a snapshot of where every individual on your team stands in terms of his particular selling prowess—and where each could benefit from more effort. By way of 25 targeted questions, the ISAT™ or the SSAT™ spits out a detailed, accurate, and objective quantification of a person's selling abilities based on five key selling factors, and illustrated on individual, team, and organizational levels.

These detailed performance benchmarks for each employee are invaluable for helping sales managers identify chasms between sales skills, behavior, and results. The executive-level report correlates all the sales data from the ISAT™ or the SSAT™ with each individual's PI® data, providing management teams with a holistic view into their members and enabling management to associate natural behaviors with sales skills and training opportunities.

For example, a company may learn from the SSAT™ that its entire sales unit needs training in listening skills. It may learn that one group needs specific education in questioning skills. It may also find out that there is actually fantastic skill knowledge diversity in the personnel files, and that their training requirements are best served by individual coaching rather than group training.

Up next, employees engage in training that enables them to target those areas identified for improvement from their SSAT score. Customer-Focused Selling™ (CFS) offers salespeople the specific knowledge they need to consistently achieve better sales results, along with maximum impact and revenue growth for the company at the helm. For frontline leaders, there is a program that actually teaches them to be stronger at influencing called Influencing-For Results™ (IFR). See http://predictive success.com/training/influencing-for-results/.

Customer-Focused Selling™ is not your typical "sales seminar." In a highly interactive, adult-learning format, CFS™ is a data-driven, evidence-based sales education that employs the latest sales techniques and provides all the core competencies needed for effective consultative selling—with special emphasis on the particular areas the SSAT™ has revealed to be in need of tweaking.

With CFS™, salespeople learn how to gain trust and credibility with their intended audience, how to sell to different styles, how to uncover client needs, and how to differentiate themselves from the competition. It's an intensive two-day bout of training that's uniquely designed to be used every day, not memorized. Better yet, for every skill covered in the exercise, there's an immediate application to a real-world business situation the professionals could potentially face. This way, the power of the tool is never in question, and participants come away from the program enthusiastic and ready to apply the new information to their own customers and prospects.

This ability to pinpoint the differences in skill levels from the data in either the ISAT/ SSAT™ can have a dramatic impact on an organization's approach to subsequent training programs. Based on SSAT™ data, managers can segment their subsequent coaching sessions to make sure they're delivering the right training to the right people in the right ways.

Bell Mobility, the mobile arm of Canada's largest tele-communications company, took its sales professionals through the SSAT™ several years ago. Some six months after the test was first administered and targeted training had occurred, the sales reps completed SSAT™ retests to measure the effectiveness of their sales training in action. The retests showed an aggregate score increase of 9 percent in sales proficiency, which translated into significant business results for the Bell Mobility team. More importantly, high-margin data sales increased by 38 percent.

It's meaningful to point out that the scientific validity of the SSAT™ has been proven many times over. The SSAT™ has been administered to business clients ranging from executives to frontline staff across a sweep of countries (including to some 20,000 individuals in North America, Europe, and Asia). For ongoing results, every member of the sales teams repeats the exercise every four to six months, and the data that results is used to hold both the sales associates and the managers who oversee them accountable.

ON-ICE APPLICATION

The powers of sophisticated quantitative and statistical analysis and predictive modeling extend well beyond the boardroom, something to which long-distance speed skater Andrew Godbout can attest. Godbout, a Dartmouth, Nova Scotia native who represented Canada on the World Cup circuit in 2008, tapped into their potential by way of the Predictive Index®. With it, Godbout learned, for example, that he's particularly aggressive and assertive—qualities that serve him well in his sport. But he's prone to letting this swell of energy distract him in the lead-up to a race, crowding out his all-important strategy, and causing him to lose focus—potentially devastating for a competition in which pacing is crucial and strategy is everything. With Predictive Index®'s help, however, the skater has learned to channel these characteristics to his ultimate advantage. Thus equipped with this new self-awareness, Godbout set about exploiting his aggressive nature to gain an early lead, but tempering it before it burned him out.

"I'm a legitimate contender but this is the first time I've been in a high-stress competition with so much at stake," Godbout said during a training phase. "[Predictive Index®] is helping me prepare for that situation."

Eventually, the results of these efforts were indisputable. Godbout's training times dropped by 8 to 10 percent, and his chances of making the team jumped from 0 to 70 percent. Godbout needed to learn that he had to slow down to win races. Describing who he is via the Predictive Index® was the trick.

THE PREDICTIVE INDEX® AND THE SOCIAL PROFIT WORLD

Over the past four years, Joanne Sweers has raised nearly $30,000 and has ridden over 5,000 kilometers in the Ride to Conquer Cancer in support of Toronto's Princess Margaret Hospital's vision to conquer cancer in our lifetime. This grueling 2-day, 200-kilometer fundraising effort was made easier for Sweers by the Predictive Index®, and the efforts it lent to helping her discover that "being more aware of what drives me and what I find challenging" are good bets for developing strategies that allow her "to be the best that I can be." The increased self-awareness with which her participation in Predictive Index® graced her has helped Sweers stay focused on the sometimes problematic task of balancing both fundraising and training.

And why not? Self-awareness is a key ingredient to success in all facets of life.

TRANSITIONING FROM BOREDOM TO THE TOP

Eugene Piric was a Microsoft Canada IT expert who was serving a national Canadian bank as a paid, on-site enterprise strategic consultant. The bank was eager to employ him and so paid Microsoft $450,000 a year to have access to Piric's IT thought leadership. But Piric wasn't satisfied and longed to get out of IT. It wasn't that he wasn't well compensated, or that he wasn't earning the respect of the business side of the bank. He just felt he needed more.

A recent graduate of Ryerson University's business program and with a science degree from a university in Serbia, Piric had a zest to get into a role that was "more me." The high-detail IT world was okay, but it simply wasn't challenging him any longer.

One look at his Predictive Index® report, and you can see why. Piric's innate need to try another function is "all there in the dots." If we had the PRO or benchmark for the enterprise strategic consultant role at Microsoft, the PRO would definitely look different from Piric's Predictive Index®. The need for the persuasive people and relationships revealed by Piric's Predictive Index® was not being totally addressed in his current post. Sure, he could perform the job well enough, and if we'd conducted a cognitive test like the Professional Learning Indicator® on him, we would certainly have seen a very high score.

But the match with what he wanted to do was simply not there.

Piric spoke with the vice-president of sales at Microsoft Canada about moving into a sales role, but given that he had no sales experience, he was told to "stay on the consulting side." He would be better served and would move up faster inside the company, they said. Frustrated, Piric applied for a transfer outside of Microsoft Canada and received an assignment as a sales specialist in Microsoft's German subsidiary.

Piric blossomed in his new post and quickly set sales records that nudged him into management. When we look at Piric's Predictive Index® survey summary, we can see that he was well suited for a persuasive management sales role that was a closer fit with his true personality. Piric achieved a 137 percent attainment rate in his quotas in 2011 and also a 48 percent year-over-year growth record. As country manager for Microsoft Serbia, he is now one of the top sales leaders in the emerging markets for Microsoft Global.

This is a great example of a candidate getting into a role that "fits who they are" (and that also matched the PRO® very well). But how costly was it for Microsoft to transfer Piric and his family across the ocean when he could have been a "diamond in the rough" right here in Canada? Too bad Microsoft Canada didn't have the Predictive Index® in its business unit prior to this placement!

LEADERSHIP DEVELOPMENT AND DECONFLICTING

As renowned American psychologist and author Daniel Goleman has pointed out, some 80 percent of a manager's success is attributable to her social/emotional intelligence. And so an ability to effectively deal with conflict has a major and direct bearing on managers' success (or lack thereof).

Still, it's difficult to quantify how effective a manager is at limiting the more disagreeable aspects of his working environment. One British study found that, while 43 percent of employees don't think their managers cope with conflict as well as they might, a full 31 percent of the managers themselves believe they do.

Training appears to wield the biggest club in this arena. Some 95 percent of individuals who've received conflict training as part of their leadership development said it helped them in some way. More than a quarter of them reported that the training enhanced their comfort level when faced with the imperative to resolve a dispute, 58 percent said they now look for win-win outcomes from conflict, and 85 percent modified the way they approach conflict as a result of the training they received.

Destructive conflict need not be an endgame to organizations who watch it fester in their midst. Those companies, whose leaders understand that conflict is inevitable in any situation populated by more than one human being, and so invest the time to prepare their people for its inevitability, are primed to emerge from the encounters better off than when they entered it.

The task of cultivating one's conflict-management skills is not cause for wringing of hands and whiny despair; it is, instead, an opportunity for fanning the flames into something eminently more productive and positive.

CONFLICT 10!

- Conflicts are a fact of life. They should be anticipated in every corner of our existence.

- Conflicts won't go away if they're ignored.

- Conflicts spur strong emotions.

- Our response to conflict is always a matter of perception; individual responses almost *always* vary.

- Conflicts result in lost productivity and lost revenue.

- The act of resolving conflict enhances trust levels and reassures the parties involved in it that they can survive such unpleasantness effectively.

Every organization's most pressing objective is to maintain sustained top-line growth. The good-looking numbers that represent success on this front are, ultimately, a product of the efforts of a devoted and well-employed group of selling professionals. The more a CEO can get out of the members of its sales crew, the more successful the organization is going to be in achieving its revenue objectives.

STORIES OF SUCCESS

Robert Watson—Olympic-Ranked Speed Skater Proves Predictive Index®

Wednesday, August 7, 2013

Despite being famous for international speed skating, Canada has only a few skaters who have ascended through the ranks to achieve world championship medals. Robert Watson from Calgary, AB, is one of them. Earning his first provincial accolades in 2007, Watson has enjoyed a meteoric rise from the bottom ranks of Ontario speed skating since 2005. He won the silver medal in the 2010 Junior World Championships, solidifying his place in the select group of international medalists. At the age of 22, Watson is one of the most accomplished speed skaters in

Figure 10.1   Robert Watson

Canada (see Figure 10.1). After examining his Predictive Index® pattern, his extensive list of accomplishments makes incredible sense.

Robert played hockey at a competitive level for eight years before he decided to pursue speed skating. The speed required to be a successful hockey player was his favorite part of the sport. At his friend's suggestion, he started speed skating at the age of 14 at the Clarington Speed Skating Club. After realizing his natural affinity for the sport, he pursued his goal of competitive skating at the Olympic Oval Calgary—training grounds in Calgary for skaters with aspirations to represent Canada in the Olympic Games.

Unfortunately, in the aftermath of being selected to compete on the Junior National Short Track Team in 2010, Watson began to lose focus on specific goals. He felt he had peaked in this area of the sport, and sought a new athletic challenge. When a former roommate offered to coach him in long track, he enthusiastically seized the opportunity.

Watson's Predictive Index® pattern supports his success as a long-track speed skater. The results of his Predictive Index® survey reveal that he is unhurried and deliberate at a fundamental level. His stability and tendency to approach tasks using established processes support his capacity to execute well on the track every time. Watson is also extremely dependable and consistent—ideal characteristics for an aspiring Olympic athlete. The sportsman has always been successful in training programs due to his methodical, steady, and even pace.

Watson's ability to listen, communicate, and collaborate with others makes him easy to coach and train. As a particularly talented listener, he requires time and cooperation to digest, practice, and adapt to change. He is extremely effective in situations that require frequent contact with others, communicating and collaborating, and understanding different viewpoints. Friendly and service-oriented, he strives for the greater good of his group, promoting teamwork and sharing authority.

Watson is extremely happy with his decision to switch to long-track. He has been training for long-track speed skating for one year and feels confident that he is at the right place in his athletic career. To stay competitive, Watson trains every day. Biking and imitations are the two primary focuses in his training regimen. Imitations are repetitive dry land exercises in which speed-skating athletes imitate specific skating techniques, repeated to achieve accuracy and consistency. In addition to imitations, Watson bikes two or three times a week to maintain his impressive endurance. His stamina is necessary—there are 10,000 meters in a long-track speed-skating race.

Watson's Predictive Index® pattern and accomplishments indicate that he is moving in the right direction as a potential Olympic long-track speed skater. His patience, work ethic, and determination predict his future success.

Look for him in the Canadian jersey in 2018. We are extremely confident in this athlete's ability to reach his Olympic goals.

―――――――

MAKING THE PERFECT PICK

High-performing individuals and the successful companies over which they preside are no accident. Neither is it luck that these entities have enjoyed the victories they have over the course of their ascending lifetimes. They are, instead, examples of the thoughtful application of the latest and most effective tools available for improving the quality of output at a professional organization.

The bottom line is this: The world is an increasingly complicated place to hang out these days. Innovation percolates at such a fantastic pace and is disseminated so instantly and pervasively, that keeping up with it all is just an extraordinary expectation. Indeed, the abundance of *choice* out there right now could be regarded as a tyranny for an individual who'd sooner drown in its depths than navigate a way out. Given this backdrop, it's more vital than ever to choose from among the plethora of business improvement tools prudently, and to apply them exceedingly carefully to one's own purposes.

Because, along with the profusion of drivel that exists inside the load of company-enhancement options at the modern business leader's disposal, there are some real gems. Pick them perfectly, and they will, in turn, help you to pick everything else more perfectly, too.

CONCLUSION:
HOW TO FINISH

Great is the art of the beginning, but greater the art is of
ending.

— Henry Wadsworth Longfellow

REMEMBER THAT PHOTO PROJECT YOU UNDERTOOK, that vast
undertaking you planned, to digitize every print from
every album in your house for—you know, the one you
got to 1977 in? What about the one where you were going
to refinish the basement floor to look like a chessboard,
for which you spent $122 on those cans of black and white
paint you're forever tripping over in the laundry room?
And what of the vegetable garden you started digging out
behind the garage three summers ago?

Rotten tomatoes, the lot of them.

Everyone knows it's a far sight easier to start a project
than it is to finish one. Your chest thrumming with enthusiasm, your head spilling over with visions of the pitch-
perfect end product, it's a sincere rush to dive into a new
venture. You sketch out the plan, you buy the supplies, you
take the first exhilarating steps into its accomplishment.

But then something shiny captures your attention and,
next thing you know, your enthusiasm has waned and

you've abandoned your lofty pursuits (and all of the expensive supplies you bought in aid of them) in favor of something else altogether.

There are dozens of tips at the ready offered by well-meaning individuals who'd like to help you see through what you started. From advice about estimating your resources smartly, budgeting your time realistically, and sidestepping your perfectionist tendencies mindfully, there's no shortage of wisdom on how to finally tie up all those dangling threads that threaten to obstruct your view.

But perhaps before mastering the art of finishing what you started, especially as it relates to hiring the right people and building the best teams, managers should first achieve an understanding of what it takes to administer a project in the first place. Only by identifying those elements of an endeavor that set it up most productively for reaching an eventual point of satisfactory completion can an employer reasonably hope to achieve the same.

INTERGENERATIONAL MANAGEMENT

For the first time in modern history, the workforce is composed of four generations of employees: traditionalists (born before 1946), baby boomers (born between 1946 and 1965), generation Xers (born between 1966 and 1980), and millennials (born between 1981 and 2000). Because each generation came of age in a distinct era, each comes loaded with its own perspective on such critical business issues as leadership, problem solving, communication, and decision-making, with the latter pair consistently ranking as the biggest intergenerational problem areas.

While these differences can drive creativity, they can also introduce a variety of challenges to a working environment that's already saddled enough with punishing competitive and economic pressures. According to a study by Lee Hecht Harrison, 60 percent of workplaces claim to be suffering the woes of intergenerational conflict.

Understanding the events and influencing factors that have shaped each generation provides a helpful context for a company keen to extract itself from this scene, but it still doesn't provide managers with enough clarity to understand and predict any individual's workplace behaviors. The range of diversity here is simply too wide.

But companies that are able to tap into behavioral data to understand their workforce at the individual and group levels will position themselves in a markedly better situation for hiring, developing, and retaining future talent. Those proven and scientifically valid approaches that measure behavioral drives and personal motivation have been proven to provide valuable, actionable insight into the five most common workplace behaviors that influence performance. They are:

Communication: Does the individual tend to connect quickly, or not so quickly, with others?

Decision-making: What is the individual's comfort level with risk?

Team participation: Does the individual tend to be more task- or people-oriented?

Action orientation: Is the individual more proactive or more responsive when it comes to taking action?

Taste for delegation: Does the individual prefer to delegate, or be delegated to?

As workforce dynamics continue to become ever more global, businesses can stay ahead of the curve by leveraging behavioral analytics to plan for both current and future workforce needs. High-performing organizations are creating competitive success by leveraging behavioral assessments to improve employee engagement, productivity, and ultimately retention with their multigenerational workforces.

———

IDENTIFYING YOUR PINK DOLPHINS

Twelve years ago, Dr. John Wang, a new PhD (biology), identified a small group of 100 pink dolphins living in the shallow rivers on the west coast of Taiwan. Since Taiwan has been slow to protect these endangered species, biologists predict that their end is in sight. There is an increased need for research so the international world can understand the critical condition of these beautiful and graceful creatures.

Without an objective and science-based plan, the demise of the pink dolphin is a certain outcome. Recent work shows us that data can be a friend to these endangered species. Researchers and scientists can use data to produce change. A company we worked with recently spoke about its own "endangered species," namely, the retiring mid-level managers. In fact, this organization went right ahead and labeled this company cohort the "Pink Dolphins." We worked with them to start piecing together a data-driven and workforce analytic approach to create a true inside grid for the next group of "Pink Dolphin" leaders. Here, we were interested in identifying who, from the individual contributor level, has the right drives, behaviors, and cognitive aptitude to fit the job model (their job PRO) for leadership roles. We took the analogy further and were in fact able to get senior leaders to think about succession planning and the identification of their future human assets as "Pink Dolphins."

In our work with leading companies, we increasingly realize that it is far less expensive to be proactive than it is to be reactive in the world of talent generation. These organizations are on the hunt for their next generational talent with an evidence-based process. Being able to spot the "Pink Dolphins," those rare and special future leaders, reduces talent costs, prepares the company for accelerated growth, and increases shareholder value.

EQ: THE MISSING LINK IN EMPLOYEE TESTING

"Studies have shown that a high emotional quotient (or EQ) boosts career success, entrepreneurial potential, leadership talent, health, relationship satisfaction, humor, and happiness. It is also the best antidote to work stress, and it matters in every job — because all jobs involve dealing with people, and people with higher EQs are more rewarding to deal with." So said Tomas Chamorro-Premuzic, a professor of business psychology at University College London, in his *Harvard Business Review* article, "Can You Really Improve Your Emotional Intelligence?"

Wow.

Such a resoundingly positive endorsement of the stuff explains why the most competitive firms are increasingly making efforts to incorporate EQ testing into their standardized assessments of candidates and current employees. Companies searching for high-performing individuals are less inclined to limit their assessment to cognitive intelligence. EQ plays an integral role in developing strategies for identifying future business leaders through supplementing conventional intelligence assessments with personality tests.

Predicting management ability is becoming an important requirement for companies that are under pressure to select the best and brightest candidates to drive growth and profitability objectives. Instead of relying on basic statistics to make hiring decisions, the EQ approach incorporates the screening of applicants for traits the firm has previously detected in successful employees, such as leadership ability and teamwork.

The Predictive Index® and Professional Learning Indicator® provide managers with the opportunity to obtain a more detailed understanding of inherent communication styles in their workforce. Empathy, from our experience is the "new black" in leading others. Are you able to understand their views, their orientation to the world? Often, it is a strong intuitive understanding of others that complements social awareness of situations (in combination with a requisite IQ) and defines an individual's likelihood of succeeding or failing in a position, especially in sales roles. Ultimately, companies are developing an increasing need for their people to have greater self-awareness — they want them to improve their ability to manage emotions and influence others.

In this way, the exhibition of management talent in a particular position is dependent on *both* cognitive ability and personality. People making hiring decisions have developed the habit of "going with their gut," or letting personal feelings compensate for the most subjective determinant of hiring decisions — an individual's personality. The use of the Predictive Index® and the Professional Learning Indicator® as tools helps managers understand personality characteristics as definitively and scientifically as they understand intelligence scores. Combining the Predictive Index® with the Professional Learning Indicator® provides organizations with the ability to match promising candidates with the best positions in order to realize high returns on employee selection.

The consideration of EQ, too, when assessing applicants also provides a solution to the problem many new professionals and students encounter: the skinny resume.

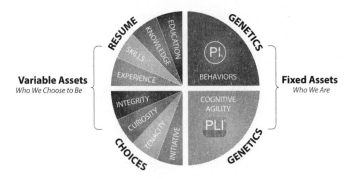

Figure C.1   The Skinny Resume® Solution.
Source: *www.predictivegroup.com*

Previously, it has been the habit of companies to judge applicants on the breadth of their experience, rather than depth. As a result, many of the best-suited candidates are overlooked because of their "shallow" resumes (see Figure C.1.).

The objective of using the Predictive Index® and the Professional Learning Indicator® assessments is to transform the way people hire and accept applications. Identifying rising stars for particular positions (for example, a student position in a high-level business program) requires evaluation of more than the extent of an applicant's experience or cognition. Utilizing personality and emotional intelligence tests provides institutions with a more comprehensive metric to evaluate a candidate's true potential.

NECESSARY ENDINGS

There is a new science to leadership. If business leaders can read one book as they prepare for their next fiscal year, it should be Dr. Henry Cloud's text, *Necessary Endings*. Dr. Cloud is a pioneer in uncovering a topic pertinent to the vitality and growth of both leaders and organizations. Every single component of life is comprised of endings; in order for something new to develop and grow, something has to move on, change, or end. Sometimes, these endings are the next natural step in order to ensure continued development, growth, and success.

Why is it so challenging for business leaders to liberate themselves from old practices and outdated strategies? Dr. Cloud uses the perfect analogy of a rosebush; some branches need to be pruned in order to make way for the "vibrant, fully mature blooms." Dr. Cloud explains that it is imperative to trim back the average, unhealthy, and dead branches that take up space needed for the healthy buds to blossom. This genius analogy is not about cutting costs or fearing failure; it's completely about sustainability and collective growth. Business leaders need to ensure that every single business decision comes from a forward-thinking place of "focus, mission, purpose, structure, and strategic execution."

How do you determine if a branch needs to be snipped? Recently, I had a conversation with a sales leader in Halifax and he specified that the best indicator of necessary change is past behavior. He highlighted the value in always moving forward, escaping stagnant positions, and using past patterns to predict and prepare for performance. You cannot expect a different outcome if you do not modify, move, or end something. One of our core beliefs is that there should be no surprises with team members, especially with regard to performance. Underperforming roses that eat away resources need to be trimmed to sustain and develop the mature blooms. From a personal perspective, we have previously had non-performing consultants prune themselves when they have realized they have stopped providing value. As Dr. Cloud puts it, this season has passed and it needed a necessary ending.

What are you doing to prune (change/alter/move/end with a strategy) those outdated practices, strategies, and wrong fits? Remember, as Dr. Cloud explains, "Your next step always depends on two ingredients: how well you are maximizing where you are right now and how ready you are to do what is necessary to get to the next place." If you have the right people and the right strategies in place, and if you eliminate or modify underperforming rosebuds — if you *pick* your flowers well — you'll be in a position to move forward and continue to grow, develop, and succeed.

INDEX